Landscapes and Gardens for Historic Buildings

Landscapes and Gardens for Historic Buildings

*A handbook for reproducing and creating
authentic landscape settings*

Rudy J. Favretti
and
Joy Putman Favretti

American Association for State and Local History

Nashville 1978

Library of Congress Cataloguing-in-Publication Data

Favretti, Rudy J
    Landscapes and gardens for historic buildings.

    Bibliography: p.
    Includes index.
    1. Historic gardens—Conservation and restora-
tion.   2. Historic sites—Conservation and restoration.   3. Landscape gardening.   4. Landscape
architecture—United States—History.   I. Favretti,
Joy P., joint author.   II. Title.
SB467.F38   712'.6'0973   78–17200
ISBN 0–910050–34–1

*Publication of this book was made possible
in part by funds from the sale of the
Bicentennial State Histories, which were
supported by the National Endowment for
the Humanities.*

Contents

Preface

UCH emphasis and care has gone into the restoration or reproduction of historic buildings. Many have been restored to a precise date or period. Others have been preserved to express transition through the years, each room representing a different period. Large sums of money have been expended to sheath the buildings authentically or to mix appropriate paints for both interior and exterior decor. Other detailed projects are performed to make the structure conform to the period or periods reflected.

This same type of in-depth restoration does not often go into the landscape setting for buildings. Modern landscape schemes and inappropriate plant material so often surround historic structures. Fences are sometimes of modern style while walkways are twentieth-century concrete. In other words, grounds do not usually show the same degree of care and thoroughness in restoration that the buildings do, and the two do not work in unison to present a total picture.

We espouse the philosophy that the grounds are just as important as the structure. If the landscape does not present a picture similar to that of the structure, you are telling an incomplete or false story, thus betraying the unsuspecting visitor. It is unfortunate that in many cases landscape parcels surrounding a historic building have been sold for other uses. It becomes even more important, then, to treat what remains in a manner that conforms to a period and style that befits the structure.

In this handbook we will use four terms in reference to the settings for buildings. The first is *garden*, which specifically means an enclosed space for the intensive growing of flowers, fruits, herbs, and vegetables. However, in some cases, we may use the word in the English sense referring to "the yard" or the space immediately surrounding the house.

The second term is *yard*. Americans have adopted the word *yard* for the terrain encircling their houses, but historically they have divided this parcel into specific spaces, for example, dooryards and barnyards. We will not use the word *yard* without its definite prefix.

A third word we will use is *grounds*, referring to the lawn adorned with trees and shrubs surrounding a building. And lastly, the term *landscape* will mean the collection of gardens, yards, and grounds into one broad scene.

It is important to realize that styles in American landscapes did not change abruptly. While we have divided this handbook into precise periods, we hasten to point out that these periods blended one into another. Also we did not break these broad periods into subperiods (such as romantic, picturesque, etc.) because such terms tend to confuse and have no real meaning. Periods in garden design are not like those in clothing and architecture. They are slow to change and oftentimes linger on for centuries.

We intend this handbook to be useful in helping you decide which landscape is correct for the building you are restoring and how to proceed in developing and maintaining that landscape. Therefore, we have divided it into four major sections. The first contains a description of the various periods in American garden design, the second tells you how to decide which period you will select and how to proceed with developing plans, the third deals with authentic plants for landscape restoration, and the final section is about maintaining the landscape and dealing with modern problems.

1

American Landscape Design

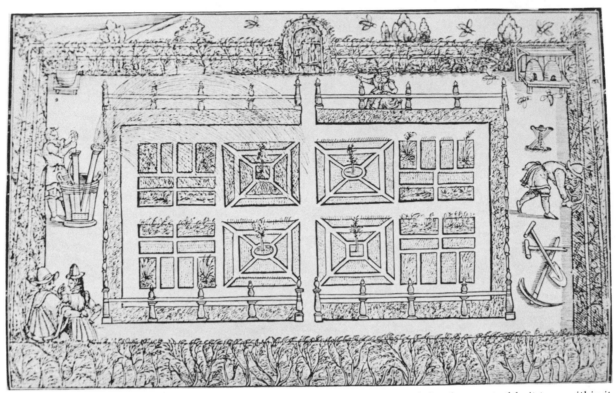

Fig. 1. *A garden of the Tudor period. Note the symmetrical bed arrangement and the placement of fruit trees within it. Also observe that the beds are subdivided with paths in a geometric pattern. The whole garden is enclosed by trained plants and the beds are set off by a rail with ornamented finials on each post.*

$\mathfrak{P}$ERIODS in American garden design closely follow those in Europe, especially those of England. When our earliest settlers arrived on American shores they brought with them a garden style to which they were accustomed and a style that, in its basic form, had been used since gardening began.

The Colonial Period, 1620–1775

Ancient Style

The formal or geometric style of gardening harks back to ancient times. As the ancients thought about growing plants, it made a great deal of sense, as it does now, from the standpoint of planting, cultivating, and harvesting to set them out in neat little blocks with paths between for easy access. Creative minds probably began making designs with the paths producing neat geometric forms. Later, as a place to obtain or store water, a well or cistern was placed as a focal point in the center or at one end of the garden.

This style probably began before recorded history and continued through the Dark, Middle, and Medieval ages to the seventeenth century. In fact, during Elizabethan times, a description of gardens would closely parallel that stated above. Perhaps gardens were more ornamented in that the boards used to raise beds were decorated and at intervals were set with posts with elaborate finials on top. It also became fashionable to create places for people to sit within the garden.

In these early gardens, fruit trees were often incorporated into the center of each garden plot or around the edge of the garden border. Here were grown tree fruits as well as bush fruits. Vine fruits, such as grapes, were trained on arbors and trellises. These often sheltered sitting places.

When our ancestors came to America, it was logical that they should carry this style of gardening with them. The style was an out-

Fig. 2. *Houses in St. Augustine showing the tightness of the spaces between structures that led to symmetrical garden plans.*

growth of gardening in tight rectangular spaces between buildings. Our early settlers also placed their gardens within enclosures so the plan with which they were so familiar was ideal. The plan was also ideal for maximum production in a small space. Lastly, new garden styles are not developed by struggling immigrants, but by wealthy landholders with ample leisure.

Almost without exception, a strict, formal, austere, geometric pattern prevailed throughout the colonies. Even the Dutch who settled New Amsterdam used the same approach in laying out their gardens, and it is said that

12 theirs were more geometric in design than those of the English.

The focus of these early American gardens was the dwelling place. Care was taken in selecting the proper setting for the house based on functional rather than aesthetic reasons. It was exceedingly important to site the house where drainage was good and where there was a good source of water. Also, it was desirable to have surrounding fields of high fertility. In fact, the development of the earliest colonies followed areas of most fertile soil as plotted today on our modern soil maps.

Other buildings, such as the cowshed, woodshed, hay barn, were sited functionally as well. In colder climates, the larger outbuildings were placed so that they would shield the house from the prevailing winds. This means that they were generally located to the northwest of the house. Plan after plan of seventeenth- and eighteenth-century settlements reveals this scheme. In the summer, the southwest breezes would carry away the barnyard odors without affecting the house.

In warmer climates, outbuildings were functionally sited but in a symmetrical manner so that they would please the eye. In their placement, there were larger spaces between

Fig. 3. *View of an old Dutch house on Long Island, New York, 1699. Note the topiary to the right of the door as well as the variety of fencing materials.*

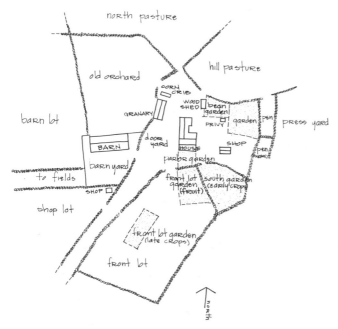

north pasture

hill pasture

old orchard

CORN CRIB

WOOD SHED · bean garden

GRANARY

PRIVY · garden pen

press yard

barn lot

door yard

HOUSE

SHOP

pen

BARN

parlor garden

barn yard

front lot garden (fruit)

south garden (early crops)

to fields

SHOP

shop lot

front lot garden (late crops)

front lot

north

Fig. 4. *A typical northern-climate building arrangement whereby the structures form an enclosed dooryard and the outbuildings protect the dwelling from the northwest winds.*

buildings because there was no need to place the buildings close together for wind protection.

We can easily see that in these plans there emerged an open space between outbuildings and house. This was referred to as the dooryard. It is from this word that *yard* evolved, meaning the space surrounding the house.

The dooryard was also an arrival space, similar to a courtyard but not always as stiff and rectangular in outline. Fences or walls connected each building so as to form a perfect enclosure, and a gate was constructed across the open end of the dooryard. Within the space itself, hogs were butchered, grains were winnowed, wagons were repaired, pumpkins were heaped, oxen and horses were shod, wood was chopped, and every kind of agricultural project that needed to be done close to home was performed.

A portion of the dooryard, usually separate from the rest but not always fenced off, was devoted to household chores. Here, for example, clothes were washed and dried, soap was made, wool was dyed.

Dooryards were no place for flowers and shrubs. While animals were not purposely kept in them, they did stray through, and chickens scratched their living in dooryards. It was not a good place to grow plants except for a few flowers in a tiny fenced plot next to the door. Daylilies, hollyhocks, or other hardy perennials found their spot along the foundation, but we may conclude that dooryards were not garden spots. Shade trees, on the other hand, were essential elements in dooryards. They were not only needed for shade, but they were also used as places to attach pulleys for lifting heavy objects.

There were other yards as well. Some farms had press yards where apples were pressed out to obtain juice for the ever-important cider. Other places had special drying yards where clothes might be laid out (before clotheslines) to dry free of animals that might tread upon them. One farm we know of had a walled-in yard always called the "play yard" where children would be kept to play while their mother performed a time-consuming chore.

Barnyards were associated with the barn or cowshed. Here livestock was kept at night to protect it from marauding wolves. Cows were milked in the barnyard during temperate times of the year instead of being stanchioned in a shed. Hogs ran loose foraging for food. Fowl of various sorts found their keep in the barnyard, although they also strayed into the dooryard as well.

The rest of the area immediately surrounding the house was divided into gardens and orchard. Gardens for the culture of small-scale vegetables (peas, onions, parsnips, carrots, lettuce, and herbs) were quite close to the house. These vegetables were not only small

Fig. 5. *A typical dooryard, about 1849. Note the enclosed vegetable garden to the right. Also, an enclosed garden (parlor garden) in front of the house. A woodpile is stacked in the dooryard and many chores are being performed there as well.*

but could also be planted easily. For this reason, plots were selected where, first of all, the soil was fertile and rich. But the second consideration was that the plot be able to trap the early spring sun. As late as 1821, William Corbett wrote in *The American Gardener* that "the ground should be level as possible because rain will wash soil. If not possible, then choose a South facing slope. Such a slope adds heat in summer but is counter balanced by the earliness which it causes in spring."

Large-scale vegetables (turnips, squash, corn, beans, and later potatoes) were planted where the soil was rich and would retain some

moisture during the summer. Obviously, a site that did not face south and one that would stay cool was essential.

We can see that the siting of buildings and gardens did not lead to a symmetrical plan in northern climates while in the South it did. Buildings could be spread out to relate properly to the yards and gardens. In the North, buildings were clustered closer together and yards fell between. Gardens were located where they could best utilize soil conditions and exposure with little regard to axial development. (See figure 4.)

Within the gardens themselves, however,

Fig. 6. *Spaces connecting buildings were walled or fenced to form a perfect dooryard or barnyard enclosure.*

symmetry prevailed. Layouts for these plots ranged from planting blocks separated with trodden earth paths to more formal arrangements in which a central axial path with secondary side paths was paved with gravel, stone, or brick. The simplest garden was probably a series of plots, each one the size needed to accommodate the crops grown or the plantings for that week. More sophisticated schemes arranged the plots so that the walks between them lined up to form a distinct geometric pattern.

Along the outside of these plots and adjoining the enclosure there were sometimes long beds where tree and bush fruits were planted. Large tree fruits, such as apples, were relegated to the orchard or dooryard, but smaller trees, such as pears, peaches, apricots, plums, and cherries, were sometimes planted in the borders. On larger properties, where there was room for an orchard, tree fruits of any kind were rarely planted in the garden border. But bush fruits, such as currants and gooseberries, were planted there.

The diary of Daniel Read records events concerning his garden starting in 1796. Read, a prosperous storekeeper, comb manufacturer, and musician (he published *The American Singing Book* in 1785 as well as other works), was born in 1757 in Rehoboth, Massachusetts, and died in New Haven, Connecticut, in 1836. Excerpts are presented here to illustrate the type of garden scheme that was common in the seventeenth and eighteenth centuries:[1]

March 28, 1796—Planted two beds of peas.
April 5, 1796—Planted the NE Square of my garden,

1. Daniel Read's diary is in possession of the New Haven Colony Historical Society, New Haven, Connecticut.

Fig. 7. *While this butchering scene was recorded in the early twentieth century, it took place in a dooryard that was laid out by the workmen's ancestors in the early eighteenth century. It depicts the use of a dooryard for one of many farm chores.*

laying out the beds N & S. In the Easternmost bed early Turnip, next green Nonpereil Peas, next onions for seed, next Drumhead Cabbage for seed and stumps of Different kinds, next English White Potatoes, next Parsnips then Beats.

April 6, 1796—Planted second square from the North end upon the E Side of the Garden.

April 11, 1796—Employed Murray in the Garden. Made the Borders, set out Currant slips and flowers and sowed some flower seeds.

April 23, 1796—Planted Spanish Potatoes in the 2d Square from the N end of the Garden upon the West side.

May 5, 1796—Planted the third Square from the North end on the E side of the Garden.

June 2, 1796—Planted in the SW Square of my Garden the 3d bed on the West . . .

Read's diary continues with many other entries in the same vein until 1806.

We can discern from these notes that his garden was large and the plots of good size in order to accommodate the plants mentioned. It appears that he was growing all his vegetables in this one garden rather than separating the

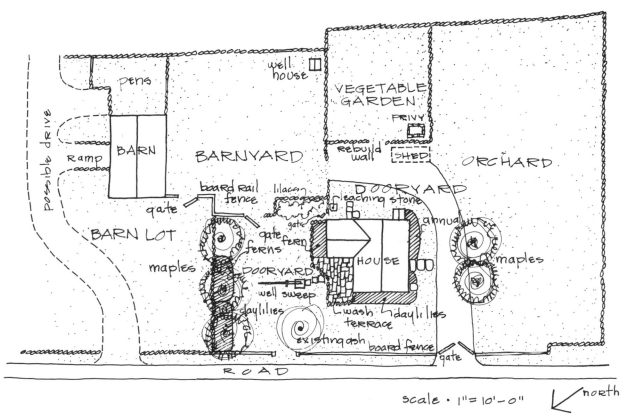

Fig. 8. *A general plan of the Bennett Farm, Hampton, Connecticut. Note the typical arrangement of the various yards, gardens, and outbuildings.*

large-scale late crops from the small-scale early crops. The latter was more common with farmers than with men such as Read who derived their livelihood from other pursuits.

We may also observe from Read's diary that he encircled his garden plots with borders for currants and flowers intermingled. Herbs were often planted in the borders or in separate sections of the larger plots.

The concept of "herb gardens," such as those we often find associated with restored houses, bears little support in the literature. It seems that herbs for medicine, cooking, or perfume were rarely set apart in a separate garden but rather grown as part of the larger garden, often in the border as mentioned above or in small plots within the central garden itself.

There are isolated cases, though, where specialization was important, and herbs were grown in separate gardens. One example is the gardens of the Shakers where herbs were cultivated for commerce. Also, some doctors kept a physic garden, often called a botanical garden. It is said that Dr. Jacobs, an early eighteenth-century doctor in Mansfield, Connecticut, kept a botanical garden so that he would have the proper herbs to cure his patients. Another instance is the sage garden, a little circular bed of sage, kept by Delia Williams in the

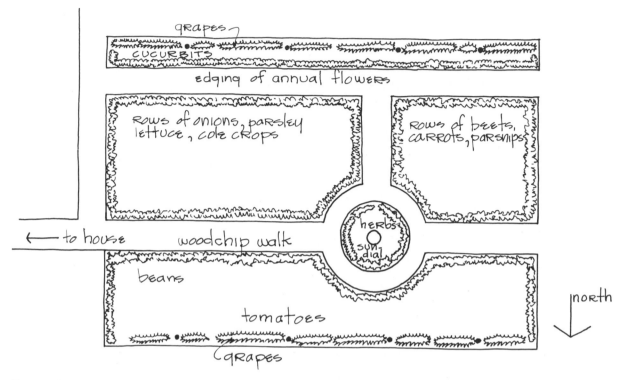

grapes

CUCURBITS

edging of annual flowers

Rows of onions, parsley lettuce, cole crops

Rows of beets, carrots, parsnips

← to house

woodchip walk

herbs
sun dial

beans

tomatoes

grapes

↓ north

Fig. 9. *The authors' vegetable garden following an ancient plan. This plan was recently adopted to increase yield and to make maintenance easier through the incorporation of the many paths.*

nineteenth century. This little garden, probably eight feet in diameter, was not far from her cheese room so that she could easily pluck sprigs to crumble and incorporate into her cheese.

Another account of a garden plan laid out in the bed or plot manner is found in *My Grandmother's Garden and an Ancestral Orchard*, by Mary Mathews Bray. The book was written in 1931, but the garden described was laid out in the early nineteenth century. We present the following description to illustrate that this style prevailed well into the nineteenth century.

The garden was enclosed by a high board fence on two sides. Currant bushes enclosed the other two. The fence was higher than a child's head. Eight square beds were in the

center of the garden. Two wide borders ran along the fence. Graveled paths were laid between beds, and the beds themselves were raised by boards.

There was no special design or arrangement of the plants within the beds. "In those days a garden was not usually arranged for the effect as a whole . . . each plant was cherished for itself, and was put where it seemed best for it individually, or often, of course, where it was most convenient." Shrubs and tall plants were placed in the borders encircling the central plots. These borders contained lilacs, roses (damask and sweet brier), asparagus ("for looks"), hollyhocks, and foxgloves. The borders were edged in boxwood, ribbon grass and moss pink.

"In our garden, according to the custom of

the times, four beds were given to herbs useful in cooking or for household remedies." The remaining beds were devoted to flowers. The four corners of one bed were filled with fleur-de-lis (iris), white and blue. The corners of another bed contained sweet williams. Honeysuckle grew over a trellis by the doorway that led to the central garden path.

We may gather from this description that the geometric scheme of ancient times prevailed into the nineteenth century, and while it was used originally for growing edible plants, it later was borrowed for growing flowers or a mixture of flowers, herbs, and vegetables.

Notice that the beds were described as being raised by boards. This was a very common practice in years past. It was believed that if the plots were raised at least six inches, the soil within would have better drainage and aeration. There is scientific truth to this practice, although during dry periods the soil is apt to dry faster. In the earliest years of our nation, before sawmills became established and when there was still much to be done to clear land, saplings were used as curbing for the raised beds.

All of these early gardens were enclosed. In the earliest years, palings were cut for this purpose. There are several entries in the Diary of Thomas Minor (1671), of Stonington, Connecticut, concerning "fetching pales" to build fences. He also notes the planting of hedges: "we made the hedge at the watters side." Enclosures were necessary to keep gardens safe from roaming livestock. Towns in this country were passing laws concerning fines on roaming

Fig. 10. *A stump fence, associated with land clearing and the enclosure of fields and pastures. This scene is Chittenango, New York.*

20 livestock as late as the 1850s, though it was considered slack agricultural practice to allow livestock to roam in built-up areas.

Fences were of three major types. First there were variations on the paling. The earliest form was probably a pointed sapling driven into the ground or affixed to a cross member with binding. A sophisticated version of this type of fence is sold today and called stockade. Variations on this fence type evolved to solid boards nailed to cross supports either with straight or pointed tips called pickets. Then pickets were varied and small spaces were left between each pole. The spaces were never wider than the breadth of a chicken.

Horizontal rail or board fences were another type. These, too, were placed with narrow spaces between. Later versions of these fences were painted white, but early ones were raw unplaned and unpainted boards, and the very earliest ones were probably saplings.

In stony terrain, as stones were cleared from fields they were piled into walls. The walls nearer the house were built neater and better than those encircling fields, though this was not always true. In the North, high brick walls were not common or even recommended because of the microclimatic situation that resulted. "Walls are some defence where they are tall and the garden Little. But otherwise

Fig. 11. *A collection of paling, board-rail, rail, stone, stone-and-rail, and picket fences in East Haven, Connecticut. Note the garden on the right.*

Fig. 14. *A cottage and garden on the Boston Post Road in New York. Notice the large trellis.*

without their shading the garden plots that existed on the sides of walks that ascended from the harbor's edge.

Another Boston garden was that of Gamaliel Wayte. It contained delicious fruits, probably planted around the circumference of the garden, and it also contained "many flowering plants." Many other Massachusetts gardens, such as those of the Endicotts, Vanes, Bellinghams, Faneuils, Hancocks, and Davenports, followed the central axis plan, and this axis even extended up fairly steep hills. The houses were sited either close to the street or, more often, with a garden in front. The central walk started at the street, went through the house, and then continued up the sloping rear terrain. The topography was often so steep that the

garden had to be terraced with fine walls. On either side of the central walk, broken by steps because of terracing, were garden plots on each level. These plots abounded with flowers, fruits, and vegetables while trees and shrubs grew in the borders along the outside. Flowers grew in the front garden on either side of the walk.

The garden of Thomas and John Hancock on Beacon Hill in Boston was large and extensive. Many of the beds in this garden were edged in boxwood, a practice very common in the South but not as common in the North where the temperature drops low in winter and the raging winds of March devastate the box. Only in seashore areas, such as Boston, would boxwood survive. Flowers grew in the box-

24

Fig. 15. *The Bryan Garden at Colonial Williamsburg, Virginia. The typical central axis, terminated by a feature (in this case a bench) forms the basic plan of this garden. Mirrored beds, edged with boxwood, border the central walk. Note how the beds are planted with groundcover, rather than flowers, to reduce maintenance. Also observe the use of fruit trees at the borders of the garden.*

edged beds, and fruit trees, among them mulberries, occupied the remaining space.

The idea of a garden to the front of the house was very common in the Northeast, not only for the elegant houses in Boston but for the simpler country places. These tiny gardens were just the width of the house and extended two-thirds that width towards the front. A usual path ran down the center, and flowers were planted on either side. Sometimes there were secondary paths branching from the central axis. These little parlor gardens were entirely devoted to flowers and shrubs because they evolved in the eighteenth century when the strict need to grow utilitarian plants was not as great.

In the cities, houses were generally built on the street on a fairly large lot. This arrangement was quite common in Philadelphia. One such garden was Clarke Hall, built about 1700. It was laid out in the old style with plots on one side of a central walk mirrored on the other side.

In the South, houses were sited on a spot of ground that offered the best prospect, usually high ground. Very little tampering was done to

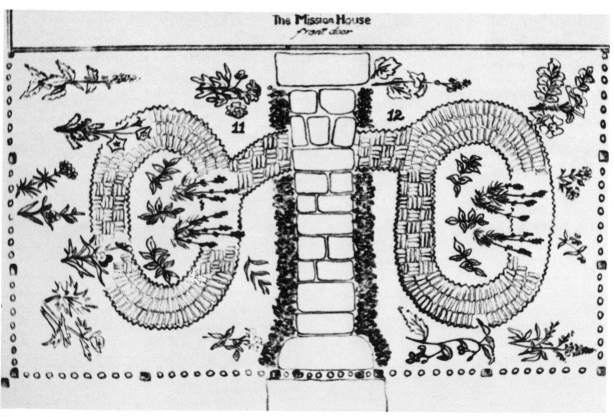

Fig. 16. *A plan for a front dooryard or parlor garden at the Mission House, Stockbridge, Massachusetts. The garden is enclosed by a picket fence. A walk of flat stone connects the gate entrance to the front door of the house. The rest of the enclosure is planted with flowers, and secondary walkways of brick branch from the main walk. These walks were often stone, grass, gravel, or trodden soil.*

Fig. 17. *The Abbott House, near Providence, Rhode Island, showing its front or parlor garden enclosed by a picket fence. Notice the board fence at the right.*

the natural slope of the land. The general plan was expansive rather than intensive because of a more favorable climate. Long axial vistas were characteristic, and tall walls, often of brick, were built for privacy and as enclosure for these gardens. Symmetry in the placement of buildings was quite common. Mount Vernon is an excellent example of this arrangement. (See figure 22.)

The Natural Style

In early eighteenth-century England there emerged a style of garden design called the natural style. It was a reaction kindled by politics, economics, art, and literature to the geometric gardens of the past.

During the late seventeenth century, English gardens took on many Dutch characteristics, possibly because William of Orange brought with him many ideas from his homeland when he married Mary. Gardens became even more intricately geometric, and statues and topiary were dotted throughout. It was this type of garden that many of our ancestors knew and which is so beautifully exemplified by the gardens behind so many of the houses at Williamsburg.

Alexander Pope, however, began writing about these gardens and satirizing them. One of his famous essays pointing at the abuse of topiary amongst his contemporaries appeared in the *Guardian* and an extract follows:

Fig. 18. *Topiary, a strong Dutch influence, used in this Williamsburg eighteenth-century garden.*

28 ADAM and *Eve* in Yew; *Adam* a little shatter'd by the fall of the Tree of Knowledge in the great Storm; *Eve* and the Serpent very flourishing.

THE Tower of *Babel,* not yet finished.

St. GEORGE in Box; his Arm scarce long enough, but will be in a Condition to stick the Dragon by next *April.*

A *green Dragon* of the same, with a Tail of Ground-Ivy for the present.

N.B. *These two not to be Sold separately.*

EDWARD the *Black Prince* in Cypress.

A *Laurustine* Bear in Blossom, with a Juniper Hunter in Berries.

A Pair of Giants, *stunted,* to be sold cheap.

A Queen *Elizabeth* in Phylyraea, a little inclining to the Green Sickness, but of full growth.

ANOTHER Queen *Elizabeth* in Myrtle, which was very forward, but Miscarried by being too near a Savine.

AN old Maid of Honour in Wormwood.

A topping *Ben Johnson* in Lawrel.

DIVERS eminent Modern Poets in Bays, somewhat blighted, to be disposed of a Pennyworth.

A Quick-set Hog shot up into a Porcupine, by its being forgot a Week in rainy Weather.

A Lavender Pig with Sage growing in his Belly.

NOAH's *Ark* in Holly, standing on the Mount; the Ribs a little damaged for want of Water.

A Pair of *Maidenheads* in Firr, in great forwardness.

Pope, as well as many other writers, was very influential among a circle of wealthy landowners. They had already been taken by the paintings of Poussin, Lorrain, and Salvator Rosa which depicted Italian landscapes containing classic temples, informal groupings of trees, rivers and streams, cattle grazing, and craggy mountains.

Soon ancient gardens were being transformed into natural landscapes of several hundred acres. Formal gardens including flowers and hedges were removed in favor of informal groupings of trees. Streams and lakes with undulating shorelines were featured rather than octagonal or circular lakes and rectangular canals. Informal paths meandered through the grounds, and a belt road lined with trees planted informally encircled the estate. Fortunately, some ancient style gardens remained for us to study today.

Along the meandering walks were placed classic temples. It may seem strange that temples were included in a natural landscape, but even those artists mentioned above believed that a mere painting of a landscape would not stand alone so they included temples in them. These temples contained busts of philosophers and heros of politics and battle. There were places in which to sit, and their contents offered inspiration for thought and conversation. (See figure 19.)

Other features of these natural landscapes were grottos or artificial caves in which people could sit. These were built of beautiful stone and shells which were often not indigenous to the site. The grotto at Pains Hill, Surrey, had several chambers, and one of these was so large that it could seat over 100 people in banquet. Within these grottos trickling water and statues were placed. (See figure 20.)

Cascades were also a feature of many of these English landscapes. These were built at the edge of a large lake or between two lakes, or even part way along a stream, such as that along the River Styx, so called, in the Elysian Fields at Stowe, Buckinghamshire. These cascades were not just a piling of rocks. They were beautifully built and elaborate structures.

Some of these "pleasure grounds" also contained hermitages, and resident hermits were hired to inhabit them. It was their job to make themselves visible, but not too much so, when visitors passed by. They were not allowed to cut their hair, trim their nails, or shed ragged clothes. Hermits lent another natural aspect to the landscape.

Some pleasure grounds contained outdoor theaters. One of the most magnificent of these is the one at Claremont, also in Surrey. It dates to the 1720s and is built into a steep hillside. It is a series of circular terraces cut into the slope

Fig. 19. *Stourhead, in Wiltshire, England, laid out by Henry Hoare between 1743 and 1776. It consists of a "natural" landscape surrounding a large lake encircled with gravel paths and roads. Notice the temple, one of several, in the landscape.*

and planted with grass. The theater is probably 200 feet across and the hill is about 50 feet high. This theater overlooks a lake that was originally perfectly round, but later made informal with an island in the center. It is believed that these theaters were places in which to sit and admire the landscape rather than places to watch theatricals.

Animals were brought into these landscapes to make them appear even more natural. Deer and peacocks were the most common, but domestic animals such as cows and sheep were also considered desirable. So that these animals would not ravage the grounds, fosses or ha-ha walls were built as a means of confining them to the outer edges. Ha-ha walls are built into a cut in the natural slope so that they cannot be seen from a vantage point within the pleasure grounds. The walls are high enough so that animals cannot surmount them. By having a ha-ha there is no need for a fence or high wall to obstruct one's view to the surrounding countryside. A feeling of expansiveness thus results. (See figure 21.)

The gardens just described were called pleasure grounds in England because they were designed purely for pleasure rather than for growing plants. For this reason, they should probably not be called gardens, though outside of England they are often called the English Landscape Garden.

Obviously, not every Englishman had this

Fig. 20. *The grotto at Stourhead. It contains a large statue of a river god emerging from the water and also a statue of a sleeping nymph. Both of these sculptures are in alcoves off a large central room.*

type of garden. It was only the very wealthy who could afford them, though wealthy but conservative gentry held on to their ancient style gardens. Also, unless its owner had a vast acreage, it was impossible to create natural landscapes with large groups of trees, lakes with meandering shores, and wandering paths and roads. Curvilinear designs do not lend themselves well to a confined space.

There are several names associated with the design of English landscapes. One of the earliest is Charles Bridgeman who worked on the ampitheater at Claremont and also introduced the ha-ha wall to Stowe when it was transformed from a geometric to a natural "garden." William Kent, an artist and architect, interpreted Lord Cobham's ideas and created the Elysian Fields, also at Stowe. The

Elysian Fields are a portion of the grounds through which a stream runs, named the River Styx. Beautiful and gentle slopes surround the stream and amid informal groupings of trees are temples and an exedra, containing many busts of ancient philosophers and British worthies. These features had much political and philosophical significance and were so placed to inspire thought and conversation. Farther along, in another part of the grounds, were other temples where visitors might sit and talk.

While Kent was working at Stowe, the gardener there was Lancelot Brown. Brown soon acquired the principles of Bridgeman and Kent and after Kent's death became far better known as a designer of landscapes. Brown further banished the use of flowers and shrubs

Fig. 21. *A typical ha-ha wall or fosse. Notice how the line of the natural topography is broken from only the top of the wall (left) to the edge of the fosse (right). From a distance, viewing across the fosse, one would not realize that the topography was broken; yet animals would stay confined because of the large ditch or fosse and the abrupt wall. Location: West Wycombe, Buckinghamshire, England.*

and reduced the landscape to a few simple elements, playing one against the other. These were bodies of water, groups of trees, and grass. He used these to great advantage to create marvelous effects of light, shade, and perspective. While his landscapes were large and magnificent, he reduced them to their simplest forms. He generally used just five species of trees, and the lawn ran right to the foundation of the house. Gardens near the house were removed. Within his landscapes, deer and cattle continued to graze.

Brown was considered extreme by some of his contemporaries and many later critics.

After Brown's death, Humphry Repton assumed his role. While Repton followed Brown's basic principles, he, too, eventually thought that Brown was too severe, and he began to create garden terraces near houses and to break down the concept of a belt road surrounding the property. It is said of Repton that he combined "all that was excellent in former schools . . . consisting of the union of artistical knowledge of the subject with good taste and sense."

With Repton, we begin to see gardening coming back into the landscape. He was an artist and was able to create picturesque scenes

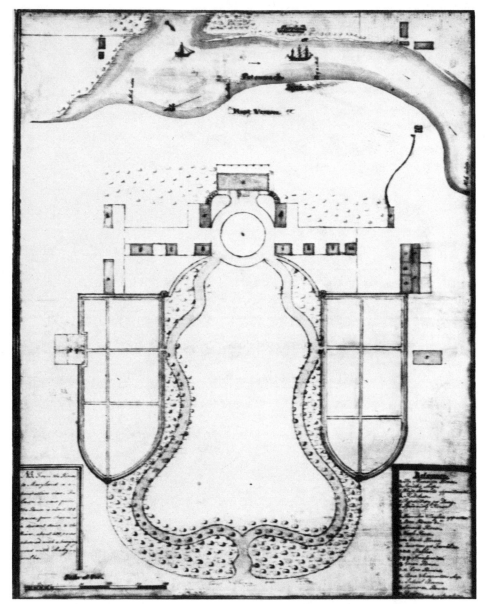

Fig. 22. *The Samuel Vaughan plan of Mount Vernon, 1787. The plan shows a symmetrical arrangement of buildings and gardens with less formal plantings of trees on either side of the main house. The bowling green widens as it leaves the house, and the walk surrounding it is bordered by plantings of trees and shrubs. The landscaped portion of the grounds is separated from the rest of the estate by the garden walls and ha-ha walls.*

in the landscape, utilizing features other than trees, water, grass, and the natural topography.

All these landscape designers, however, adhered to the rule that in designing a landscape the place itself should dictate a plan for the grounds. In other words, the designer should follow the dictates of the topography and the various natural features of the site. To quote Pope, one must "consult the genius of the place. . . ."

The natural style was brought to this country by Washington and Jefferson through their readings and Jefferson's travels abroad. An analysis of the plan for Mount Vernon shows an undulating though symmetrical shape for the bowling green, and it is known that Washington had a deer park on the river side of his mansion. The animals were kept from the bowling green and the immediate lawn about his house by a ha-ha wall.

At Monticello, Jefferson employed many of the elements of the English landscape garden. His gardens on the west front of his mansion surround a serpentine walk that is irregular in design. Groupings of trees formed a transition between the lawn and his grove of eighteen acres in which he had deer. He projected a grotto, some temples, an extensive cascade, but it is believed that these were never built.

Fig. 23. *Monticello, showing Jefferson's west lawn surrounded by a round-about walk, edged with flower beds. The entire west lawn (including the walk and flower beds) was enclosed by informal plantings of trees and shrubs.*

34   Gardens of the New Nation, 1776—1850

Washington and Jefferson set the stage for the natural style in America. But other gentlemen designed or redesigned their properties along the same principles as well. One such estate was Belmont near Philadelphia. Within this landscape there were summerhouses and a wilderness of trees, though several of the ancient features were retained such as a parterre garden and avenues of trees.

Solitude was another Philadelphia estate, the seat of John Penn, established in 1784. The house was situated on a rise of ground with

fine vistas to the surrounding countryside. The landscape was encircled by a ha-ha wall and there was a large informal tree planting east of the mansion. This landscape followed many of the principles of Brown, but undulating flower beds near the house suggest a Reptonian influence as well.

The seat of William Hamilton, also near Philadelphia, and named Woodlands, was another example of pleasure grounds in America. Hamilton corresponded with Jefferson exchanging ideas about his landscape. He also collected many exotic trees which he grew in an informal manner on his estate.

Claremont, the estate of Chancellor

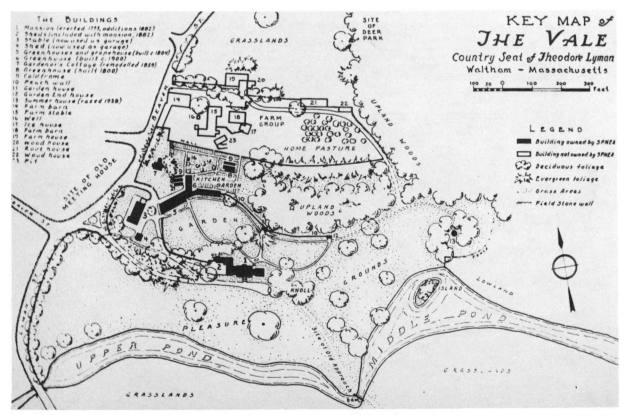

Fig. 24. *Plan for the Vale, Waltham, Massachusetts. Observe the pleasure grounds, including a summerhouse, in the lower part of the plan. The garden, to the rear of the house, is asymmetrically laid out and defined by a long "peach wall," against which tender fruits were planted for ripening. The kitchen garden is in the old style.*

Livingstone along the Hudson River in New York, displayed a perfect English landscape, complete with a lawn undulating with water, magnificent vistas, and informal woods.

On the shores of the Hudson River were other fine examples of the *jardin anglais*. One more such place was Hyde Park, the seat of Dr. Hosack. His landscape contained many features of a pleasure ground, including deer.

One of the finest examples of a pleasure ground in New England was the Vale, the estate of the Lyman family in Waltham, Massachusetts. A deer park was an important part of this landscape, and the grounds were enriched with plantings of English limes (lindens), elms, oaks and many other trees and native plants. There are still fine old examples of trees planted in the 1790s growing on the estate.

Another excellent Massachusetts landscape is Gore Place, the home of Christopher Gore, established in 1786. These grounds were developed in the true English landscape style but probably not until the second house was built in 1799 after a disastrous fire. The grounds have a "Mile-Long Walk" encircling them, and there was also a ha-ha wall on the place, suggesting that animals grazed on the adjacent fields. A variety of trees were informally planted on the grounds.

These are but a few of the estates along the eastern seaboard that were planted in the English landscape style. No doubt there were many others, though there is a reason to believe that this style was never as prevalent as it was in England. In fact, the eminent English horticulturist, J. C. Loudon, in his *Encyclopedia of Gardening* (1834 edition), states: "Landscape gardening is practiced in the United States on a comparatively limited scale; because in a country where all men have equal rights, and where every man, however humble, has a house and garden of his own, it is not likely that there should be many large parks [meaning landscaped pleasure grounds].

The only splendid example of park and hothouse gardening that, we trust, will ever be found in the United States, and ultimately in every country are such that will be formed by towns, villages or other communities, for the joint use and enjoyment of all inhabitants or members."

Loudon, known to be interested in promoting public parks for industrial towns in England, was certainly prophetic in forecasting the great American park movement, started by Andrew Jackson Downing and later so magnificently carried forth by Frederick Law Olmsted. Public parks in America started to be established within a few decades of this prophecy, and it was in these American public parks that most of the elements characteristic of the English pleasure grounds were installed for the pleasure of all.

Much of the American landscape that had been settled was in farmland, except for the portion under villages and cities. Pastures and fields, with copses of trees growing in them or along the many streams and rivers, gave much the same effect as the English landscape. Our ancestors found themselves surrounded by pastoral beauty, but its reason for being was not necessarily aesthetic as was the case with English pleasure grounds.

Joseph Loudon developed a style of landscaping which he called gardenesque. This meant that flower beds, shrubs, and combinations of trees and shrubs returned to the landscape and became the most important elements, but not in rigidly symmetrical patterns. In fact, he said, "Wherever symmetry is useful to the mind, and may assist its functions, it is agreeable: but wherever symmetry is useless, it becomes distasteful, because it takes away variety. . . ." Loudon was quoting Baron Montesquieu with these remarks. (See figure 34.)

Loudon, then, returned horticulture and the growing of plants to gardens of England. Actually, they had never been abandoned in

36

Fig. 25. *View of Sharon. Note how the countryside is open, pierced only by groups or thickets of trees, quite reminiscent of an English landscape.*

Fig. 26. *An oil painting (1796) of Mrs. Judson Canfield, by Ralph Earl. Artists of this period often included natural landscapes as background or as scenes through an open window.*

this country. His influence, coupled with the emergence of numerous seed houses and nurseries, set the stage for gardens to come in the nineteenth century. Plant explorations from American shores also helped this movement along as did wealth derived from increasing industrialization. In the nineteenth century, America enjoyed its "golden years of horticulture."

Bernard McMahon, an Irishman turned American, established a seed house in Philadelphia in 1796 when Loudon was only thirteen years old. Later, in 1806, McMahon published the first major book on horticulture and landscaping ever published in the United States. He called it *The American Gardener's Calendar*. It was long a standard and popular work. Thomas Jefferson is known to have had a copy in his library.

While most of McMahon's book concerns itself with horticulture, there is an important section within its covers that deals with landscape design, basically following Reptonian principles.

McMahon advocated siting the house on a summit of ground so that it might have a good prospect for its inhabitants to enjoy. He felt that a house so located is a healthier place in which to dwell. He also felt that the grounds around the house should be laid out in a natural style, with the land consulted for clues as to how it should be treated.

He went on to say that formal designs had almost been abolished, such as square grass plots, parterres, long straight walks, regular intersections, quadrangular and angular spaces, and "other uniformities as in ancient design." Instead he advocated "rural open spaces" with green grass ground of varied dimensions and winding walks, all abounding with plantations of trees and shrubs and flowers in various clumps.

McMahon's idea of a grass lawn in front of the house, widening as it leaves the house's walls, and enframed by "thickets" (meaning masses of trees and shrubs), is Reptonian in

quality. In fact, this was one of Repton's trademarks which he used to satisfy clients who had tired of Brown's severe treatment. The lawn at Monticello is an example of this type as is one of the proposed designs for the Elias Hasket Derby House by Samuel McIntire. (See figure 27.)

McMahon advocated openings in the tree and shrub planting surrounding the lawn so that vistas to the surrounding ground could be seen. He further suggested that a serpentine walk be made surrounding the lawn with branches going off into adjoining compartments or spaces. These walks were to communicate with the house so that people would be attracted to them.

In addition to outlining the walks with plantings of trees and shrubs, he also favored planting the boundaries of the property. Recesses were to be left in these thickets for grottos, temples, and statues, and he warned that it was important to leave vistas through the trees.

The design of tree and shrub thickets varied a great deal from the way we design shrub borders today. It is now our custom to use large masses of the same species and to repeat these masses at intervals, always taking care to maintain a proper balance and seasonal effect. In the early nineteenth century, the scheme was to place the tallest shrubs in the center of the rear of the thickets. These tall shrubs were often pointed evergreens, such as cedar and spruce. Surrounding these pointed trees were shrubs, tiered down to an edging of flowers. (See figure 28.)

The shrubs used were of various species, not large masses of one kind. Most of them were deciduous because the common evergreens such as those we use today were not in common use. These thickets were probably so called because there was a great unevenness in their overall appearance and because of the variety of shrubs used, quite like a natural thicket. (See figure 29.)

While McMahon abolished parterres as the

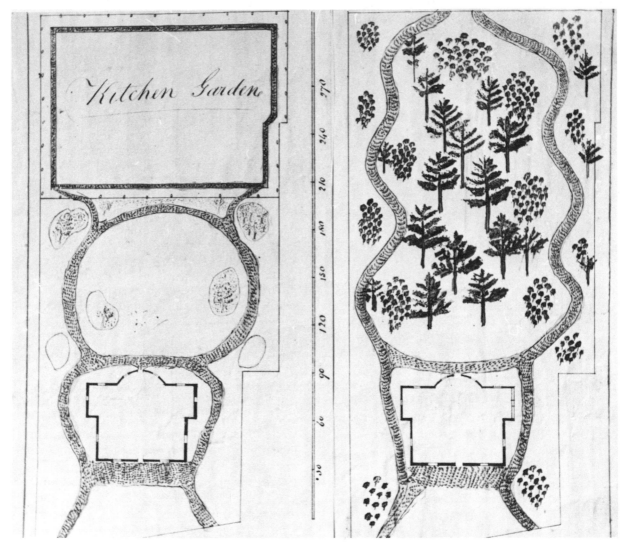

Fig. 27. *Two garden schemes drawn for the Elias Hasket Derby Mansion, Salem, Massachusetts, by the famous architect Samuel McIntire, who designed the mansion. Both these plans follow the trend of the period toward an informal lawn arrangement, surrounded by a walk or path, and informally planted with trees and shrubs. McIntire also drew a third suggestion that was more traditional and symmetrical in nature.*

Fig. 28. *A grouping or thicket of shrubs with pointed evergreens in the center of the shrub mass.*

Fig. 29. *A shrub thicket showing a variety of plant species and forms rather than just a few as used today.*

40   main feature in front of the house, he did advocate them in a secondary place, perhaps in a hedged or shrubbed compartment, as a place to grow flowers for enjoyment. He also felt that the clumps of shrubs planted to define the lawn should be edged with flowers. Other portions of the grounds might be devoted to a "wilderness" of irregular plantings, with walkways penetrating this wilderness, either of grass or gravel, taking off at odd angles and interwoven with the plantings.

    Except for the parterre compartment for growing flowers, we gather that McMahon's landscape was entirely informal with curving lines throughout. But he does mention that for contrast, and where appropriate, "straight ranges of trees" might be used, deciduous or evergreen. At Andrew Jackson's Hermitage, we find a fine example of a "straight range of trees" in the cedars that are planted in front of the mansion. McMahon also suggested that other compartments might contain a maze or a labyrinth.

    Where appropriate, he felt that water should be used. Streams trickling through the site, or ponds or lakes, should be made a major part of

Fig. 30. *As shrub thickets matured, the pointed evergreens in the center tended to outgrow the rest of the mass. This lithograph of Judge Ingraham's residence in Harlem, New York (1858), also illustrates the edging of shrub thickets with flowers or low hedge material (see right of center). This raised house is also typical of architecture in certain regions of the South.*

Fig. 31. *A stately row of cedars at the Hermitage, near Nashville, Tennessee. "Straight ranges of trees" were often used to add a majestic note and to contrast with the rest of the landscape. Jackson's range of cedars was supposedly planned by the artist Ralph E. W. Earl. They fan out in the form of a guitar as they approach the house.*

the landscape, and where possible, cascades should be constructed. Also, if it was possible, he specified that a mount should be built. A mount is a building placed on a mound of ground where people may sit and view the scenery.

From these brief comments on McMahon's principles of landscape design, we may conclude that most of what he advocated had its roots in the English natural style, further refined by Repton and then promoted by himself. He felt, however, that these principles were slow to take hold. He stated in the preface to an early edition of his book that "America has not yet made the rapid progress in gardening, ornamental planting, and fanciful rural designs, which might naturally be expected from an intelligent, happy, and independent people, possessed so universally of landed property, unoppressed by taxation or tithes, and blessed with consequent comfort and affluence."

McMahon died in 1816. His book passed through eleven editions, read by many and practiced in principle.

In 1841, a twenty-six-year-old man by the

42 name of Andrew Jackson Downing published another book called *A Treatise on the Theory and Practice of Landscape Gardening*. It was the first book entirely devoted to the subject, and Downing acknowledged in it that he followed the ideas of both McMahon and Loudon.

While Downing advocated the same basic style, there are a few differences in his recommendations. For one thing, he placed greater emphasis on laying out an approach road to the house. He felt that this road should not be a direct route and that it should meander slightly, without being impractical, so that vistas could be enjoyed at intervals as one

approached the house. He did advocate "mingled borders" at the edges of a lawn, however.

In addition to being a nurseryman and the first real landscape designer in this country, Downing, along with his associates, also designed houses for his landscapes. He believed that Gothic, Italianate, and Tudor styles blended best with the peaks and ridges of mountains and trees, and for this reason most of his designs were of these types. In other words, the towers, roof peaks, and chimney stacks of his proposed structures echoed the same "points" in the landscape. He abhorred

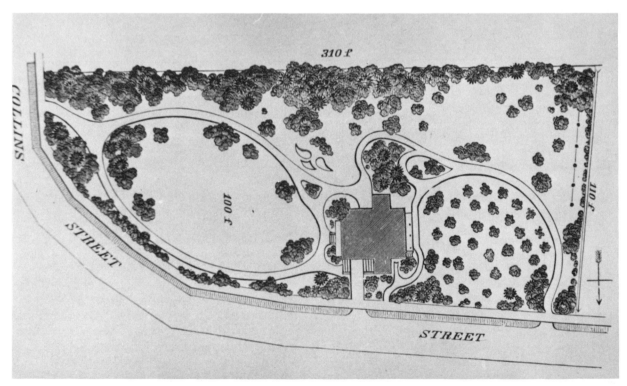

Fig. 32. *Plan of house and grounds showing several typical landscape features. Note approach driveway designed to present the best aspect of the house and to be as long and pleasant as possible without being awkward. The boundaries are thickly planted with thickets of trees and shrubs. The tear-drop forms in the lawn near the house are flower beds. To the rear of the property is an orchard. Note that the various parts of the landscape are defined and divided by trees and shrubs, a concept advocated today.*

Fig. 33. A sketch of Andrew Jackson Downing's house in Newburgh, New York. Observe the use of pointed evergreens (picturesque) to echo the architecture of the house. Also note the specimen round-headed trees. Flower beds containing a minimum of flower species were sited near the house. Also, vases (urns) on appropriate pedestals were strategically placed in the landscape as sculptural elements, but not filled with flowers.

the Greek Revival or classical style because it did not do this sort of thing and also because he felt such floor plans were impractical.

In the South, where Greek Revival was becoming popular, Downing's proposed architecture did not take hold as it did in the North. McMahon and Loudon seemed to be the leaders in the landscape movement there through their printed works. In the North, however, numerous places were built and planted following Downing's designs, which

were regularly published in the *Horticulturist* that he edited for several years.

Downing situated his houses in a spot with good prospect, and around the house he planned a lawn. Circular flower beds were to be built in the lawn and near the dwelling house so that they could easily be seen by the inhabitants and their visitors. Also, during the summer months, fragrance could enter through the windows. He did not advocate foundation plantings of any kind, though

Fig. 34. *The plantation doctor's office at Rosedown, St. Francisville, Louisiana, showing a gardenesque landscape treatment. Note the emphasis on gardens containing varied plant material as well as a flowing walk system from which to view and enjoy the plantings.*

sometimes he did suggest shrubs in circular beds. Urns, which he called vases, were also a part of the adornment near the house, and they were always to be placed on a pedestal rather than directly on the lawn. He cautioned against overusing urns and also against planting flowers in them "and reducing them to a mere flower pot."

He banished the planting of trees in a straight line, except for an orchard. Rather, he preferred trees planted either singly or in masses. He divided trees into two groups: the round-headed ones he called the beautiful, and the pointed ones which he called the picturesque. These were to be planted some

singly and some in groups, to achieve the proper effect. It is easy to see that the pointed trees (larch, spruce, hemlock) repeated the lines of the peaks and towers on the house and that the round forms (white oak, maple) stood "beautifully" alone.

Downing's plans also called for water where practical. He was strongly in favor of a "picturesque vale" containing a stream in which a cascade could be built and the slopes beautifully planted with shrubs and the ledges with vines. Within this landscape rustic seats were to be built where people could sit and enjoy the scenes.

Through the writings of these two men,

Fig. 35. *Another example of a Downing landscape. This property (the Beekman House, Beekman Hill, New York, on 50th Street, near First Avenue) was newly planted when this lithograph was made in 1860. However, note the evergreen trees as well as large deciduous ones. Also note the vase in the center and the fountain at the extreme right.*

McMahon and Downing, many American properties were planned and planted according to the natural or romantic style. Naturally, not everyone followed their advice. Many adhered to their existing landscapes in the ancient style. Others combined both styles. Some were too poor to change.

Apparently certain areas of the country reacted to the new style in varying ways. In the South, where plantation houses were being built in the classical style, some of McMahon's ideas were accepted, but Loudon's gardenesque influence seems to have been stronger. In an 1852 issue of the *Horticulturist*, George Jacques of Worcester, Massachusetts, wrote that "in New England . . . the laws of

taste are made to conform to the more stringent code of convenience, economy and utility. Probably more of this prevails in New England than elsewhere; for here, more than in other lands, utility has become one of the secular deities of popular worship. In this section of the country, whenever a contest takes place between economical advantage and good taste, the latter is sure to find some apology for making a hasty retreat."

The Victorian Period, 1860–1900

For decades, critics have called Victorian landscapes cluttered and overdone. Perhaps

Fig. 36. *Sundials were popular sculptural features, placed within a garden or against a shrub thicket at the edge of a lawn or near a walk path. Sundials have remained major garden features well into this century. The following poem describes a sundial in an early twentieth-century garden.*

The Sundial

Daphne plants around the base,
Storm stained numbers on its face.
Ivy clad, it stands alone
Far from pool and bench of stone,
Saying to the golden flowers:
"I count none but sunny hours."

John Rollin MacDonald, 1949

Fig. 37. *Picturesque evergreens combined with deciduous trees and shrubs. Combinations such as these were used to define a lawn area, at the edges of the property, or at the juncture of paths or roads within the landscape. They were also planted to enframe vistas or as free-standing specimen groups.*

Fig. 38. *A group of several species of deciduous trees and shrubs.*

Fig. 39. *A rustic seat in an alcove of shrubs.*

this was true in some instances, but in gardens of good taste it was certainly not the case. It is true that during this era line and form were exaggerated. Plants with large, coarse-textured leaves became popular. Double flowers gained broader acceptance than in the past. Garden urns were cast ornately rather than with the classical lines of the early nineteenth century. Even within flower beds, intricate patterns were made with flowers.

Taste was affected by wealth derived from great industrial development. Also there were other reasons for this change in garden design. In previous eras, there were but a handful of nurseries and seed houses. Perhaps the most famous early nursery was that of the Prince family in Flushing, Long Island, started in 1737, but there were few others until the late eighteenth century when Landreth and McMahon started their seed houses and nurseries in Philadelphia in 1784 and 1806. Seed houses emerged in New York, Boston, and other populated centers, but through the nineteenth century nurseries and seed houses burgeoned throughout the country. During the period of China trade, many fine oriental plants were introduced into the new nation, and sea captains continued to import exotic trees and shrubs throughout the nineteenth century.

Fig. 40. *A rustic seat with an appropriate shrub background.*

Lewis and Clark essentially started an era of plant exploration that expanded greatly, so that by the late Victorian period, organized plant explorations to the Orient and other parts of the world were finding many new species for American gardens. Arboreta and botanical gardens contained these collections from which cuttings were released to nurseries for general sale.

Thus American gardeners had a varied palette of plants with much new and exotic material. While deciduous material of a simpler growth habit was quite common until this era, we now begin to see bold-leaved evergreens and large-leaved perennials, as well as trees with new and interesting leaf patterns for use in Victorian gardens.

Garden designs during the Victorian era changed little from those of Downing earlier in the century. Perhaps more fountains and urns were used as ornaments in the lawn and certainly flower beds became more "mingled" with plants. Gardeners did not follow the Downing principles of keeping the variety of plants within circular flower beds restrained. Instead, designs were made with plants of the same height, and this was called carpet bedding.

There were many types of carpet bedding. Some consisted of geometric designs simply

Fig. 41. *A raised bed planted precisely with concentric rings of uniform plants which probably possessed foliage of contrasting colors. Note the large single plant for emphasis at the pinnacle. This is but one design for a carpet bed. Designs were as varied as the whim of the gardener and the availability of plants. The beds were raised to show off the design and also for drainage.*

laid out in a circular or rectangular bed that was slightly raised in the center so that the design would show better. Other times, these designs were laid against a slope of ground to really show them off. In other cases, the configuration of the bed was in the form of leaves and stems. These were quite popular. In still other cases, baskets of flowers and sundials were planted against a slope using plants for all elements within the design except for the gnomon in the sundial.

We must not leave the impression that every Victorian landscape had a carpet-bedded garden, because maintenance for these gardens was extremely involved. First of all, a greenhouse was required to grow all of the plants. It took great horticultural skill to grow them (see the plant lists starting on page 155) so that they would all be of the same size and

shape. In other words, a skilled gardener had to direct such a project and its maintenance. We may conclude that this type of garden was installed primarily by the wealthy and copied on a limited scale by others.

Carpet beds were imitated by people of lesser means, but often not with great skill. Most elaborate designs appeared in the many city parks that had been established in the last half of the nineteenth century. These carpet beds served as a great incentive to park strollers. The following article entitled "Pimples on Nature's Face," appeared in an issue of the *Ladies Home Journal* in 1908, during the declining years of Victoriana:

The Gardeners of our Public Parks have much to answer for. Very soon their annual hideous work will show forth. Beds of hyacinths and tulips of precise geometric exactness in the form of zones, of

Fig. 42. A carpet bed with ribbons of plants forming the design. Note that the bed was raised in the center and that an accent plant was planted on the mound.

circles, stars, triangles, squares and elipses will blossom forth, and thousands will admire and exclaim. And, worst of all, they will go and do likewise on a smaller scale in their own gardens, or when they have them. And a hopeful anchor of "Dusty Miller," edged with clam shells, will be cast against a terrace like a railroad station embankment; stereotyped beds of screaming geraniums will cut up a lawn (and we may well be thankful if in the same bed are not planted some pink geraniums, as does the skillful New York City public gardener at Union Square). And if we are spared the owner's initials in party-colors, we are fortunate! It is not so surprising that a woman recently asked her gardener to lay out on her beautiful lawn a baby elephant made of cactus rosettes, and when her husband questioned the expediency of it she took him by the hand and showed him a life-sized elephant so constructed on the greensward of the City Park! How far away from nature do we depart when we so insult the flowers, the grass and our neighbors! Why do those in charge of city parks allow this unintelligent formality, this stereotyped monotony and this insincerity of gardening to go on, with the result of the miseducation of our people? With a people in such crying need of gardening as we Americans are, it is really nothing short of criminal that such excrescences are allowed on the green lawns of our parks—veritable pimples on the face of Nature.

Fig. 43. *A form of carpet bedding utilizing rattan and metal to make the basket which is then planted with flowers. This bed is built against a slope.*

Fig. 44. *Carpet beds were especially associated with parks and certain public and government buildings. Here is a carpet bed at the White House in the late nineteenth century.*

Another aspect of Victorian landscapes was the emergence of elements from many landscape styles—French, Italian, Classic, and Oriental. Parterre gardens, definitely French in spirit, became extremely popular as layouts for rose beds. Boxwood-edged beds formed the parterre design and the areas between were filled with roses. In this sense, they were not true parterres because the design made of edging plants should have been the most dominant feature of a parterre. (See figure 46.)

Some gardens contained an abundance of statuary and water cascades reminiscent of the gardens of Italy. Balustraded terraces entered the scene, especially on sloping sites, just like those ancient gardens near Florence and Rome. Classical elements, such as columns, exedras, and the ever-present vases and urns gained their place in the garden along with large terra-cotta pots.

Pagoda-type summerhouses were sometimes built and Japanese stone lanterns were dotted throughout gardens intended to generate an oriental feeling. Contorted and strictly pruned evergreens in combinations with stepping-stones and moon bridges (where water was present) further carried out the oriental motif. (See figure 47.)

The Victorian period was an era of eclecticism. Traditional colonial-style gardens were even incorporated into the landscape scheme. It was not unusual to have a central path garden with a gate at the end that led into a parterre rose or annual garden. Beyond that, in another portion of the grounds, might be an oriental garden. All of these on the same site. On the other hand, not every place had such a combination. Some just included plantings of shrubs around the boundaries with large specimen shade trees in the lawn. A stately approach was laid in front of the house and a fountain might have been installed either in the front or side garden.

Victorian grounds were usually fenced. Wood fences were still the most inexpensive because wood was plentiful in most regions and labor was cheap. But cast-iron fences also

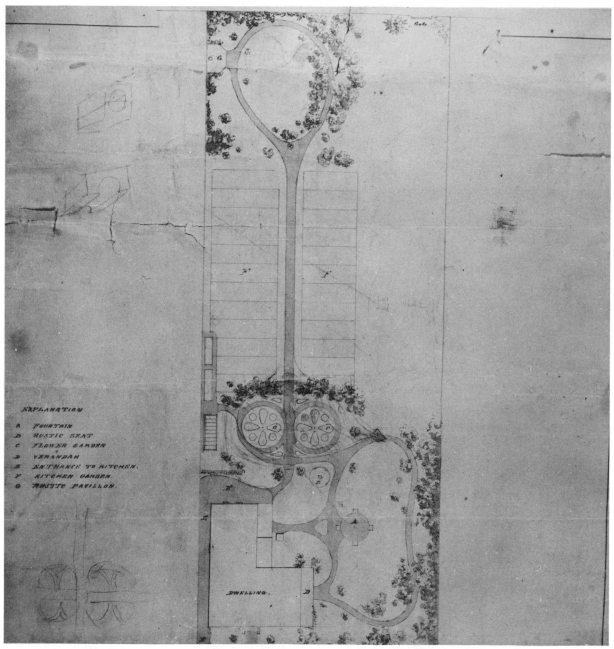

Fig. 45. *A plan of the garden at the Butler-McCook House in Hartford, Connecticut, drawn by Jacob Weidenmann, 1865. The garden was originally of the ancient, central-axis-walk type. Weidenmann revised it to include a boxwood flower parterre (c); a fountain (a); a rustic seat (b); and a rustic pavilion (g). The old part of the garden was retained with upper center (f) as a kitchen garden. A meandering walk was installed in the revised parts of the garden and typically bordered with trees and shrubs.*

54

Fig. 46. *Parterres became popular during the Victorian period. The design was made with boxwood or other hedging material. In the sense that the spaces between the hedging were planted with flowers, they were not true parterres, but rather knot gardens. These designs were sometimes used for rose gardens.*

Fig. 47. *Victorian houses in Buffalo, New York, about 1883. Note the extensive use of stately trees, both along the street and on the residential grounds. Note also such features as circular approach drives, circular flower beds, and an oriental summerhouse. Also, heavy balustraded fences appear.*

Fig. 48. *An Italianate-style house, surrounded by groups and specimens of stately trees. The landscape is extremely simple. Observe the absence of any foundation planting, quite typical of the early Victorian period. This landscape, representing the late 1850s, preceded the days of lawn mowers.*

became very popular (starting in 1830), and they increased in popularity as the century progressed. Iron could be cast into practically any design so there was great variation in the types available. The infinite variety in cast-iron fence design produced heavy-membered fences suitable in scale to large, massive houses and grounds as well as delicate designs better suited to small houses. As a rule of thumb, the heavier the design, the later in the period it appeared. (See figures 49-51.)

Cast iron was not restricted just to fences. Numerous other garden ornaments were cast

as well, such as statues for the lawn (deer, stags, dogs, lions, boars, and classical figures), fountains and urns, benches and seats, hitching posts and mounting blocks, lampposts and birdhouses. Cast-iron summerhouses sometimes replaced rustic wooden ones as main attractions in the garden. There were numerous foundaries casting all types of fences and garden ornaments for American landscapes. (See figures 52-57.)

Statues were used most as central features for gardens or as accents to garden entrances or the grounds. Urns, too, were installed

Fig. 49. *Cast-iron fence in the Victorian era.*

primarily as accents to entrances or as central features in a garden. Very large statues were sometimes placed in the center of a lawn, though this practice would have been frowned upon by designers of better taste. Fountains, on the other hand, were often placed in the lawn with a planting of low-growing shrubs, flowers, or a groundcover around their base.

As the Victorian era advanced, foundation plantings became quite popular. Large Victorian houses were set on very high foundations, and it became necessary to plant masses of shrubs along these foundations to soften and conceal them. Again, large-leaved evergreens as well as needle types were combined with deciduous material for this purpose. Variegated plants and those with colored leaves were also included for special interest. Some foundation plantings became plant collections and drew all attention away from the house itself.

Not all gardens in the Victorian period followed the grand style just described. Gardens of individuals with lesser means or those of workmen and craftsmen did not usually take on such ornate features as fountains and carpet bedding, although simple round beds on either side of the front walk or in the center of a side lawn might have been installed.

Fig. 50. *Cast-iron fence*.

Fig. 51. *Cast-iron fence*.

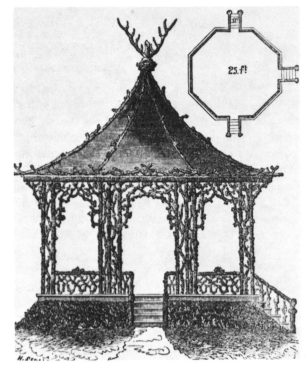

Fig. 52. *Garden pavilion of cast iron.*

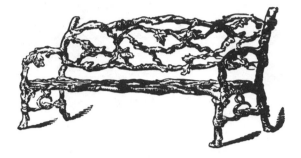

Fig. 53. *Cast-iron bench.*

Fig. 54. *Cast-iron bench.*

61

Fig. 56. *Birdhouse made of cast iron.*

Fig. 55. *Garden vase or urn made of cast iron.*

Fig. 57. *Cast-iron fountains were often central features in a garden or lawn area.*

Fig. 58. *Foundation plantings began to emerge in the last quarter of the nineteenth century as house foundations were built higher. Mixed plantings of shrubs girded entire house foundations. Sometimes masses of shrubs were set out from the foundations such as those shown in the center of this scene.*

Within the boundary fence, however, garden plans were very simple. Shrubs often edged the boundary as well as flower borders. In the rear of the property was a garden, usually quite symmetrical in layout. Fruit trees abounded in the rear yard, and a few large shade trees were included in the front if there was room. Urns were about the only kind of ornamentation that would be found in these landscapes.

In rural areas, the landscaping around the house often consisted of a grove of trees planted either in the front or alongside the house where they were most needed to provide shade and where they wouldn't cast shadows upon the garden. These trees were not always planted all at one time, but rather individually or in groups to commemorate a birth or special event. Many such groves were planted in 1876 to celebrate the centennial of this country.

Along the approach road, or in special locations in a side or front yard, circular beds containing flowers or groundcover might have been planted. Nearer the house or along a fence or wall, a mingled border of flowers and

Fig. 59. *A house in Florida (1882) showing a landscape treatment typical of the middle years of the nineteenth century. Shrubs were planted, not as an organized foundation planting, but where they would grow best or where it was felt they were needed.*

roses was often installed. There always was a large vegetable garden following the principles of the ancient style.

The Early Twentieth Century, 1900–1930

The ideas set forth by McMahon and supported by Downing continued to prevail in the early twentieth century, meaning that properties, however large, were divided into "compartments" separated by shrubs or walls. In fact, this concept is still used in modern landscaping.

The idea of an eclectic landscape was not advocated by these men. Strong eclecticism began during the Victorian era and reached its height in the early twentieth century. During that period, French, Italian, oriental, and colonial gardens were installed on larger estates. The gardens clustered around the dwelling house, and the grounds surrounding might have been planted in the English landscape style or in a "wild garden."

Gardens on several levels were in vogue, and this is why Italian gardens and architecture gained popularity. Balustraded terraces could be made on a hilly site as well as dramatic cascades and water steps, reminiscent of those in Italy. Italian gardens lent themselves very well to the use of statuary, a trademark of the early twentieth century, as well as sculptured shrubs.

Grand avenues also gained popularity, quite like those in France. Associated with French design, many parterres were installed especially as beds for roses. Large pools or canals of water, laid within a panel of green lawn and the whole outlined with trees, usually formed at least one axis of many twentieth century gardens.

The early twentieth century had as one of its distinctive features the use of very fine statuary, most of it in stone or bronze rather than cast iron. Classic figures were the most popular, and they were often placed as foci in a garden or at the end of an axis or to accentuate certain parts of a garden. Exedras, containing many pieces of very fine original works, sometimes created a backdrop for a garden.

Another distinctive feature of early twentieth-century gardens was the pergola, an Italian influence. Pergolas, usually in the classic style, but sometimes oriental or even Gothic, were set as the main focal point. Sometimes one entered a garden through a

Fig. 60. *Lithograph of the residence of William H. Smith, Saratoga, New York. It shows the house surrounded by a grove of trees, probably planted to commemorate an event. Some low-growing plants appear near the foundation. These were no doubt herbaceous perennials.*

Fig. 61. *A late nineteenth-century farmstead. Here we see a flower garden neatly enclosed by a picket fence. The whole plan generally follows the ancient scheme.*

Fig. 62. *The architectural style in garden design. Note such Italian influences as the balustraded terrace with steps between levels. A Jekyll-type perennial border is also included. The structure on the upper terrace is a teahouse.*

pergola overgrown with appropriate flowering vines or climbing roses. In some cases, pergolas were built as ruins with only the freestanding columns in place. Summerhouses, or teahouses as they were often called, continued to be features in gardens even though pergolas were most in style. They may have been placed in another garden or as a subservient feature in a very large space.

Fountains continued to be important elements in gardens of the early twentieth century. Instead of being cast in iron, most of them were stone and beautifully sculptured. As in the case of statuary, most were classic in design and less ornate than those of the Victorian period. Wall fountains and gargoyles, placed along the garden or terrace wall, were common in smaller gardens or as secondary features where a large principal fountain was the main focus.

Early twentieth-century gardens and grounds were architectural gardens, meaning that their design was highly structured and that they contained many architectural elements such as pergolas, fountains, teahouses, limestone benches, sundials, rose arches, and sheared shrubs for accent. A strong axial plan tied the gardens together.

Fig. 63. *Pergolas, also an Italian feature, were popular early twentieth-century garden features as were garden pools set into a grass panel.*

The center of the gardens themselves might have been devoted to a parterre or colonial plan. But a most popular arrangement was a panel of grass containing either a pool or sculpture. Central grass panels outlined by a walk with a large perennial border between the walk and an enclosing wall or fence were common. This type of garden was often sunken, and a terrace, usually immediately outside the house, overlooked it. (See figure 66.)

Surrounding either one or a series of these architectural gardens was either a wild garden or an English landscape, both containing groups of trees. Wild gardens contained carefully planned tree groups with wild flowers, groundcover, and bulbs beneath. This type of garden had been strongly proposed by William Robinson in Britain in the late nineteenth century and was very much in vogue here in the very late Victorian era and into the twentieth century. Beatrix Farrand, an eminent early twentieth-century landscape architect, was a master of this style. (See figure 67.)

Previously we mentioned the use of large perennial borders. By the early twentieth century, Americans had felt the influence of the work and writings of Gertrude Jekyll, famous for her designed perennial borders in which

Fig. 64. *Walls, terraces, and the resulting sunken gardens were distinctly early twentieth-century elements. These gardens were accented with numerous examples of fine sculpture.*

Fig. 65. *A fine example of an architectural garden typical of the early twentieth century. Notice the teahouse, sunken garden, walls, steps, sculpture (even topiary), and mixed perennial borders.*

Fig. 66. *Garden with a central grass panel, surrounded by a walk and perennial borders. These were quite reminiscent of the English style.*

Fig. 67. *Woodland gardens were ideal for certain sites and for the edges of many twentieth-century gardens.*

great attention was paid to color, texture, and the combination of forms and mass. Many American authors such as Mrs. Francis King, Helena Rutherford Ely, and Louise Beebe Wilder carried forth the principles of Gertrude Jekyll.

Rock gardens also became extremely important during the early twentieth century. Because it was stylish to have gardens on various levels, the slopes that intervened made ideal places to install rocks in naturalistic fashion and to tie the whole together with plants. Some rock gardens were a mixture of plants while others were specialized, containing alpines or dwarf evergreens, or some other specific plant group.

Early twentieth-century grounds were often surrounded by an iron fence or stone wall. The entrance to the grounds was accented by a magnificent gate with appropriate posts and finials. The number of entrance designs varied with architects and designers. Most were original in design while others were sold as ready-made elements. (See figure 68.)

Smaller gardens tended to follow the basic nineteenth century plan set forth by McMahon and Downing or the ancient style or a combination. Rarely did gardens on a very small site combine many European or oriental motifs. Most properties had a front yard consisting of a lawn with a foundation planting surrounding the house. Perhaps a tree or two was planted there depending upon the situation. A driveway went along one side of the property leading to a coach house or garage.

To the rear of the house, the garden may have accommodated a drying yard where a clothesline was situated. Sometimes this was concealed, but other times the clothespoles may have stood on the lawn. Lawns were surrounded by flower borders or shrubs or a fence, depending upon the taste of the owners.

Service yards, where trash cans and woodpiles were placed, were sometimes a part of the rear yard as were vegetable and fruit gardens. Trees were planted for shade if there was room, and shrub borders were used for privacy along the boundaries of the property. (See figure 70.)

Landscape Settings for Public Buildings and Spaces

In the earliest years of our nation, the primary public building was the church. It was used not only for religious purposes but also as a meeting place. Churches usually were the hub or center of a town, and if we look at old maps we see that roads seem to radiate from the church or center.

Fig. 68. *Large estates were enclosed by walls or fences that were pierced only by elaborate gates at the entrance.*

Fig. 69. *A workingman's garden usually had a grass panel, surrounded by flowers, near the rear of the house. This also served as a drying yard. The terrain beyond was devoted to vegetables and fruit.*

74

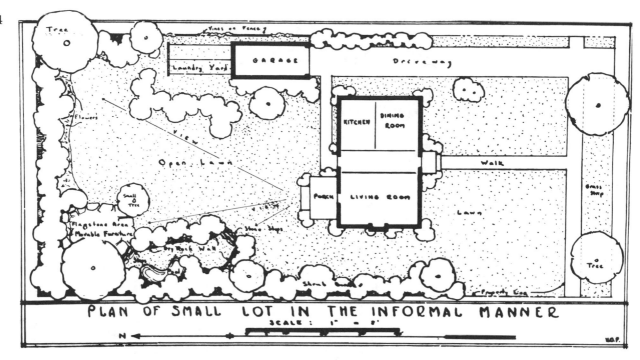

Fig. 70. *Drying yards were often screened, and vegetable gardens were somewhat separated from the rest of the site, which was then made entirely ornamental.*

Churches were usually devoid of any landscape treatment whatsoever. We have yet to see any evidence that shows planting around a place of worship save for some wild ferns or weeds that volunteered. There really wasn't any reason to landscape a church because it was used only on Sunday, and then parishioners were not out of doors. And who would care for the plantings when there was so much farm work to do? Furthermore, it might have been considered a sacrilege to ornament a sacred place of worship.

There may have been a large tree or two on the edge of the church property or near the horse shed or on the green or commons near the church. These would be necessary to shade the horses while they waited for their riders and drivers who were attending meeting. Some native trees, such as maples, pines, or

oaks, were probably left when the initial clearing was done.

Another very early public building, though privately owned, was the inn or tavern. Innkeepers were very busy people and did not usually plant an ornamental garden for their visitors. Sometimes, daylillies may have lined the foundation, or perhaps some volunteer violets. Maybe a lilac or a rose would deck the corners of the building. But we may be quite sure that in a majority of cases, no flower gardens adorned the grounds of a tavern. Vegetable gardens, on the other hand, would have been an important part of the grounds of an inn because vegetables were necessary for food for the innkeeper, his family, and his guests. (See figure 72.)

Shops, mills, and other structures where crafts were performed were sited on private

Fig. 71. *A typical austere church landscape of the early nineteenth century. Notice the planting of trees (in the left foreground) in this 1836 scene.*

land; the mills were along streams, and those shops that did not need water power were elsewhere. Mills were never landscaped in the earliest years, and for that matter very few of them were into the twentieth century, even when industry swelled and prospered.

Most public buildings such as courthouses, banks, and schools were on plots of ground not much larger than the building itself, leaving very little room even if landscaping had been the style. We know of one instance in a New England town where a piece of land 22 feet by 18 feet was given to build a school of the same dimensions. Land was not "wasted" to build these public structures as it is today.

As mentioned previously in relation to places of worship, trees were the only plants that were planted near public buildings. Longfellow tells us of the "spreading chestnut tree" by his famous blacksmith shop. Numerous early engravings show a single tree or possibly two near a bank or schoolhouse. But landscaping ended there. Trees were essential for shade, but there wasn't any need (nor was there room) to plant anything else, it was thought. (See figure 73.)

Fig. 72. *The Buck Horn Tavern in New York, built in 1812. Notice that there are no landscape plantings, except for a little side garden, associated with this structure.*

Fig. 73. *Franklin College, in Athens, Georgia. The only landscaping is large, stately trees.*

78   Street trees have had several periods of favor since colonial times. In the late eighteenth century, there was a strong tree-planting movement throughout most of the country. Funds were raised, money was voted, and organizations were formed to plant trees in town centers and along the streets themselves. This movement continued through the nineteenth century with a great deal of success. Actually, although interest in street tree planting fluctuated somewhat depending on the times, trees were planted extensively until the mid-twentieth century. During the late 1940s and 1950s, few were planted. It was not until the 1960s when Mrs. Lyndon B. Johnson started her beautification movement that interest was somewhat revived.

The planting of shrubs around foundations of buildings was a late-Victorian idea. In many communities the high foundations of buildings were planted with bold shrubbery, though we cannot say that this was true in general. It seems that where there was space, school grounds were often planted at least in the front of the building. The rear was reserved for playgrounds. Libraries were planted depending upon their endowment and interest in the community. Banks were very often planted if there was space in front, but so often they were built right next to a sidewalk.

Fig. 74. *Street tree planting in Chelsea, Massachusetts. Notice that the trees are protected with wood enclosures against the damage of wagon wheel hubs.*

Fig. 75. *Many trees growing along streets were native species, such as these stately elms.*

Cemeteries

The earliest cemeteries in this nation were by necessity sited on the most gravelly or best-drained pieces of ground that could be found and as near the church as possible. It is interesting to notice that where a church sat on poorly drained soil, the graveyard was detached from it, down the road a little distance. But when the church was on well-drained soil, the graveyard was placed adjacent to it.

Our early graveyards were austere. Gravestones were set in rows, not always straight. The stones were generally quite similar save for various images engraved upon them. There were few trees and plants in the graveyard because it was often the habit to have the sexton of the church pasture his cow in the walled or fenced-in graveyard so that the grass would be kept down. Naturally, any desirable shrubs or flowers would have been eaten. (See figure 77.)

The only type of vegetation found in a graveyard might have been a shade tree or two growing along the wall. These were usually native trees, not exotic or introduced species. Brush tended to grow along the wall unless clipped out by the sexton or whoever was designated to control it.

In 1825, the Mount Auburn Cemetery was conceived in Cambridge, Massachusetts. (See figures 78, 79.) Dr. Jacob Bigelow and a com-

Fig. 76. *The Department of Agriculture Building in Washington. During the late nineteenth century, public buildings were often heavily planted with foundation plantings.*

Fig. 77. *An austere graveyard with the graves set row on row and devoid of plantings.*

82

Fig. 78. *Forest Pond, Mount Auburn Cemetery, planned and landscaped as a park. Note strolling visitors.*

Fig. 79. *The mount or tower in Mount Auburn Cemetery, which commands a view of the surrounding countryside.*

Fig. 80. *A glimpse of a portion of Central Park in 1872.*

mittee worked on the plans for this new burial place, and it was laid out in 1831. Mount Auburn Cemetery was a great breakthrough in cemetery design in that it was innovative and unlike any other cemetery before it. The reason for its uniqueness was that it was quite like a park with meandering walks (each with a romantic name) that blended with the contours of the land. On the highest spot of terrain was a mount from which much of the adjoining countryside could be viewed. Mausoleums were cleverly built into the slopes instead of standing out on flat ground. Four ponds were focal points in this cemetery, and the entire site was beautifully planted with trees.

There were no public parks in America at this time. Mount Auburn Cemetery became a park, and people flocked there on Sunday afternoons to stroll and relax. Actually, Mount Auburn Cemetery was the forerunner of the great park movement in this country. This movement gained momentum with the planning of the mall in Washington by Andrew Jackson Downing in 1852 and the planning of Bushnell Park in Hartford, Connecticut, in 1853. Soon afterwards, Olmsted and Vaux designed Central Park in New York.

2

Research and Plan Development

$\mathcal{B}$EFORE you plan a restoration, consider whether every property should have a landscape setting or a garden. Concerning public buildings, we have discussed the subject in the last section. With regard to residential properties, it is safe to assume that most had a garden of sorts. The reason is that in 1790 over 90 percent of all Americans were engaged in agriculture, meaning that they were self-sustaining. By 1850, the figure had dropped to 64 percent and by 1900 to 38 percent. By 1930, only 21 percent of our population operated a farm. The landscapes of farmers contained at least a vegetable garden and in many cases a small flower garden managed by the farmer's wife.

As the number of individuals engaged in farming declined, the number engaged in industry increased. As this increase in industry was advancing throughout the nineteenth century, so was interest in horticulture and gardening. So we may conclude that most industrialists probably had landscaped grounds surrounding their residences and that even factory workers had a small garden in which to grow a few vegetables and flowers. Perhaps this was not the case in highly urbanized situations, but in most other cases, we may safely assume that some garden existed.

Site Analysis

The first step in planning a reproduction, restoration, or re-creation is to conduct a detailed survey of the site in question and to plot all information on a plan drawn to scale. You need not be a skillful draftsman to do this. The major point is to gather everything on paper for future use in the plan development process.

All data derived through site inspection must be plotted to scale on a plan. A scale of one inch representing ten feet is ideal. Or you can allow one inch to eight feet, meaning that you can use a conventional ruler as a scale rather than buying an engineer's scale in which an inch is divided into ten parts. Certainly, the site survey that you make should not be recorded at a scale larger than one inch equals twenty feet. By plotting the whole site analysis to scale, and making every element on the plan to scale, you will get an accurate relationship of all parts of the plan.

The following items should be recorded on the plan:

1. *Property boundaries.* These are exceedingly important because they define the edges or bounds of the property. You should obtain this information from a surveyor's map. Most states require such a document when property ownership is transferred. Hence, a plot plan accompanying the original recorded deed may contain the exact boundaries of the property. (See figure 81.)

2. *All structures on the property.* All buildings (houses, barns, sheds, chicken houses, garages, etc.) must be recorded on the site analysis plan. These should be drawn to precise scale, and the windows and doorways on the first floor should also be indicated. Also, doorsteps or landings must be recorded to exact scale. It is a good idea to record the location of buildings that you know are going to be removed because the site analysis plan will be preserved and may become the only record of what was on the property when you started the restoration project. For example, you may be removing a fairly modern carport added to an early nineteenth-century house which is being restored to its earliest period. This should be shown on the site plan. (See figure 81.)

3. *Fences, walls, and elements of enclosures.* All fences and walls, be they retaining walls or freestanding, should be shown on the plan using proper symbols. Even if you are not sure whether or not they are authentic, you must

88

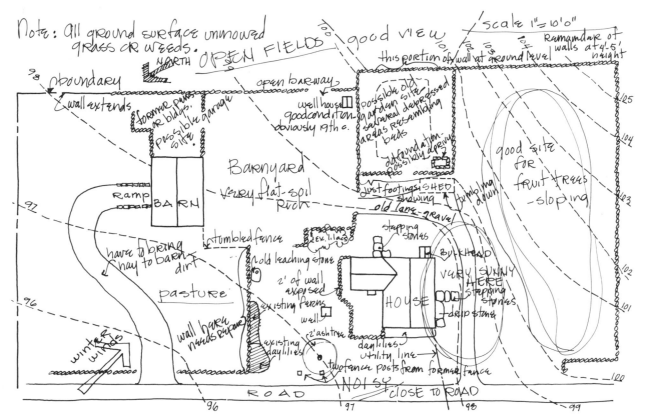

Fig. 81. *The site analysis plan of Bennett Farm (see Fig. 8). Notice that every site analysis feature mentioned in the text has been recorded to scale on this plan.*

include them at this point because the site analysis plan must contain everything you find. (See figure 81.)

4. *Walks, driveways, and all other pavement.* Regardless of whether the walks and driveways or paths are correct, record them on the site analysis plan along with an indication of materials used as pavement. You may well change the location of these elements, based on research, but record their location as you find them. (See figure 81.)

5. *Posts, bollards, poles.* Any freestanding post, bollard, or pole should be recorded be they wood, stone, or some other material. There may be just one standing post, for

example, but research may reveal that this was just part of a row or series of hitching posts that were later sheared off at ground level. An erect wooden post, partially rotted, may be the base of a hops pole or drying tree. You may discover its function by reading the diaries of past inhabitants of the dwelling. (See figure 81.)

6. *Plants and vegetation.* Record the location of all existing trees, shrubs, and perennials and properly identify them. Trees and shrubs may easily be recorded at a scale of 1″ = 10′ or 1″ = 8′ but if you are attempting to record the remnants of a perennial garden, it is better to blow up the scale of that section of the

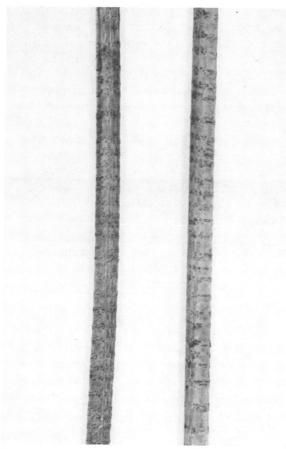

Fig. 82. *A boring of an oak tree, made with an increment borer. The annual growth rings (dark) may be counted on this sample and the age of the tree recorded.*

property to ¼″ = 1′ or 1″ = 4′. This scale will be more manageable, and when you conclude the project it will be easier to read your own notes.

All trees, shrubs, and perennials should be plotted on the plan. Some of them may indicate a pattern for future restored landscape. Make no decisions concerning what you will leave out or remove at this point except for noxious weeds or overgrown brambles that obstruct your analysis process. If you are not

sure of the identity of some plants, consult an expert who does know. These plants may then be checked against the authentic plants list starting on page 124. You may also wish to consult with a forester who may make borings of some of the trees to obtain data concerning their age. The condition of trees and shrubs should also be noted on the site analysis plan.

7. *All other specific features such as remnants of old foundations, man-made riprapping, arbors, trellises, and curbing.* These should be plotted on the plan, drawn to scale. Further research may show that some of these elements were part of the plan you intend to re-create or re-store. (see figure 81.)

8. *Site observations.* Any distinct depressions in the ground, mounds or heaps, caved-in areas, or any undulation in the land or openings in a fence or wall should be indicated on your site analysis plan. Archaeological investigations at these places (done by professionals) may reveal the site of roads, paths, walks, or previous buildings. One site on which we recently worked showed some irregularities in the soil adjoining the front of the dwelling house. Upon investigation it was found that beneath the soil was a large cobbled drip line. The soil on top was merely an accumulation of decayed leaves and plant material. (See Figure 81.)

9. *Views or vistas, within the site and without.* With defining arrows, indicate any outstanding vistas or views both within the site and off the site. It may be that you will not employ these in the final design for the property, but you should record where they are in the event that you need this information later on. (See figure 81.)

10. *Utilities.* You should also indicate on the site analysis plan the location of all utilities, such as sewer, water, gas, and electric. While these are modern conveniences, they must be reckoned with as restoration proceeds and you must be aware of their precise locations. (See figure 81.)

90   11. *All natural features* (variation in soil types, rocks, ledges, water, changes in elevation). All natural features must be recorded in the site analysis because they may well be incorporated into the final plan. If ledges are present, for example, you can be sure that they were always there and should not be removed for any new project. The same would be true of water or soil types unless these were changed through diversion during recent years. For example, it is conceivable that the development of adjoining land could affect the drainage pattern on the property in question. (See figure 81.)

12. *Weather information.* Record direction of winter winds, summer breezes, or any microclimatic information that is known, such as frost pockets that hamper early spring bloom. Sections of the tract where the sun is parching, or where no sun shines because of intense shade, should also be indicated. Naturally, the north point should be indicated on all plans as well.

13. *All other features not previously mentioned.* Because a site analysis plan should be a complete and detailed document of everything you find on a site before restoration begins, you must record all data found through general observation and detailed probing. There may be some specific items that are peculiar to the site that should be recorded, such as dump heaps, ash pits, etc. Be sure to record everything you find on the site.

Photographic Record

Each of the categories indicated above should (in addition to being recorded on the site analysis plan) be recorded photographically. Each item should be carefully photographed and any details in the structure should also be taken. Each of the other items that is photographable should be recorded in a similar manner.

You should indicate on your site analysis plan, or on another plan drawn specifically for the purpose, the angle from which each picture was taken, and these notations should be coded to the numbers on the pictures. Each photograph must be carefully numbered and labeled. The label should contain as much information about the subject as you can record.

These pictures will be useful in making planning decisions when you are not able to be on the site, and also they will serve as a permanent record of what the site was like before you began restorative work. While black and white pictures are most useful for this purpose, it is good to have a set of colored slides as well because they are helpful in giving talks to stir interest and to keep members of a group, society, or committee informed.

You need not be a photographer to acquire a photographic record of your project. Within a community, there are usually any number of amateur photographers who are more than willing to conduct a useful project provided that you pay for the film and its processing. If you are near enough to a college or school that teaches preservation, there often are classes looking for a project on which to conduct a photographic analysis.

Research and Documentation

We have listed the site analysis process first in the total scheme of research and plan development, but research and documentation may well be conducted first or simultaneously. We do feel that there is a slight advantage in conducting a site analysis before any other step is performed. In this way, you will not be influenced by any research data that you are finding in deciding what to record on your site analysis plan. But if you follow our advice and record *everything* you see, then it really doesn't matter if you do research first or second.

In the research and documentation phase,

you are seeking any information you can obtain that is recorded graphically, in writing, through archaeological investigation, or through hearsay. In searching for these kinds of information, we wish to ascertain as much as possible about:

1. The general layout of the grounds, landscape, or gardens surrounding the building in question.
2. Any details, such as plans, for any part of the total landscape.
3. Details concerning specific landscape features, such as fences, summerhouses, trellises, sculpture, sundials, hitching posts, steps, paving, plants, and related items.

4. Specific information about the people who inhabited the structure throughout the years of its existence and how the structure and landscape were used.

Graphic Records

Daguerreotypes, Tintypes, and Photographs. These are the best sources for documentation when they are available because they show an image exactly the way it was and there is less opportunity for errors through interpretation. Of course, these records did not exist until the second quarter of the nineteenth century. Care should be taken in studying these sources. A magnifying glass

Fig. 83. *Example of an old picture used as a research tool. This one shows a simple dooryard, the type of fence used, and a front garden on the left, enclosed by a fence. Also, a clothesline is evident across the dooryard.*

92

Fig. 84. *This photo shows clearly the twisted-wire fence of figure 83.*

should be used to seek detail not readily visible. Have several experts study them. For example, a plantsman can often identify plants by leaf pattern. A carpenter may be able to see particular hardware on a fence gate.

If you are satisfied that photographic material does not exist for the project in question, then study related projects of a similar period and nature. These often give clues and ideas concerning the type of setting your building should have.

Prints. Before the days of photography and even after, sketches were drawn by artists and made into lithographs and etchings and engravings to illustrate newspapers, journals, and books or to be enframed as a piece of art. Any artists' works may contain considerable license taken by the artist in his interpretation, but it is generally agreed that prints specifically done for illustration are apt to be more precise than images conveyed through paintings. Prints are extremely valuable in showing us the landscapes surrounding a building and details within the landscape such as plant forms, garden features, and the types of fences used. Sometimes they indicate garden practices. We have used many prints to illustrate this book. When you study them, you will see the many kinds of data you can derive from prints as a research source. While prints may not be available for your project, study related projects or buildings to gain ideas on how the setting should be developed.

Drawings and sketches. We have already mentioned these in our comments about prints and engravings, but now we are referring to sketches of an amateur nature, drawn in journals or diaries or kept by members of a family. We have come across numerous sketches in old family papers that have been useful in constructing certain landscape elements. One that comes to mind is a cider press, drawn by a child in an autograph-memento book. It was a cider press in her yard, and the drawing would be quite useful in reconstructing that element in a landscape. Amateurs are apt to include too much detail in their drawings, and this makes them quite useful for restoration purposes. (See figure 86.)

Maps. Maps are a useful source for determining layout between buildings and the arrangement of streets, walks, roads, and paths. While maps do not often contain minute detail (because of their scale), they do contain valuable generalities and may even show the location of major features such as trees, monuments, flagpoles, bridges, signs, and gardens. Some maps were drawn as

Fig. 85. *A sprayer of the mid-nineteenth century being used to treat the soil against troublesome worms.*

Fig. 86. *Sketch of a cider press made by Louise Billings Spaulding in the middle of the nineteenth century. It shows considerable detail.*

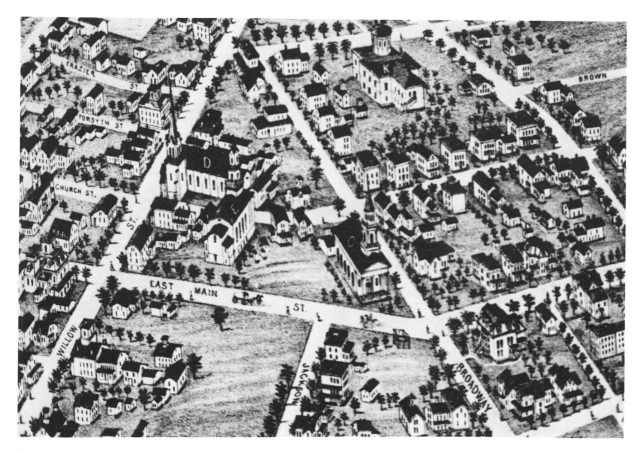

Fig. 87. *Portion of a dioramic map showing the arrangement of houses, outbuildings, and trees. Some maps show fences bordering individual properties.*

dioramic views, and these are especially useful in showing major landscape features.

Paintings. Paintings are useful guides for restoration purposes. If you know the painter's reputation for accuracy, then they can be more than guides. But it is wise to keep in mind that, especially in the placement of gardens, trees, shrubs, and plants, artists take great license and are apt to place these features where they create the best composition or improve upon the scene. For example, there are paintings of Monticello showing the mansion painted white with scattered perennials throughout the west lawn. Authorities do not believe that the mansion was ever painted white but rather that it was the artist's attempt to make the mansion look more classical. And there is no evidence that Jefferson ever scattered flower beds helter-skelter across the west lawn.

Written Records

Written records are invaluable for researching and documenting landscapes. As mentioned previously, these references leave much to the reader's imagination and interpretation,

96 but if they are written in some detail, they will reveal much needed and useful information. Often times, data derived from a written sou ce support graphic information, and thus you are able to obtain quite a precise picture. Again, you should not be discouraged if you cannot find data on your project. In this case, if you nave exhausted all possibilities, you may have to draw your landscape restoration plan based on styles for other grounds in the region.

Diaries and journals. We have found diaries and journals to be a valuable source of information not so much to provide information about a garden plan but to describe how a landscape was used. A simple description such as "washed clothes under the willow tree by the sinkroom door" indicates that there was a willow tree somewhere near that door and that clothes were washed out of doors near that spot. Through site analysis, a large flat rock near the sinkroom door with a mound next to it may suggest that the washtubs were placed on this large flat rock, and the mound is probably the decayed remains of the tree's root mass. Repeated references to washing clothes in that location suggest that the sinkroom door portion of the dooryard was the area devoted to household chores. On one project, it was through a diary that we learned that the diarist had a hops pole. Upon questioning descendants, we determined what the pole looked like (a dead cedar tree placed in the ground) and that the one pole yielded enough hops to use as a painkiller for earaches.

Diaries and journals yield all kinds of valuable information including long lists of plants grown and what plants were used for what purposes (culinary, medicinal, fragrance). For the careful researcher it is safe to say that a diary or journal, no matter how brief, will yield some valuable information about landscapes and how they were used.

Correspondence. Letters often contain descriptions of places visited or tasks performed, and these descriptions sometimes are about landscapes or gardens. Even today, though we tend to write less lengthy letters because other means of communication are better, we do write home about what we are seeing. In years past when people stayed away longer to make a trip worthwhile, descriptions were more lengthy and detailed. Unfortunately, few letters were kept and even when they were, some in the sequence were lost, so that relying on correspondence for information can be sketchy. But it is an area not to be overlooked.

Travel Accounts. There were many travelers, especially in late colonial and early federal times, who wrote extensive accounts. For example, *Travels in North America* by Peter Kalm presents much information about plants and landscapes. People also wrote about gardens of famous personalities they had visited. In fact, the more famous the person, the more there is written about his landscape.

Scrapbooks. Especially during the late nineteenth century, it was quite fashionable to keep scrapbooks containing clippings from newspapers, postcards, and a myriad of other information. Sometimes these descriptions are valuable in reconstructing a landscape scene. One such clipping we know of reads as follows: "The big two-story brick church, in general plan like the present U. P. Church, stood less than a block from the 'Pappy Williams' home, a frame cottage, overgrown in summer with vines, with two stories to the southern sun and only one to the north. It was very pleasant, our ancient editor said, to sit against the southern side, in the warm spring sun, and look out over the valley just freshly coloring with spring green." Unfortunately, like most clippings, this one was not dated or identified, but supposedly it appeared in the *Guernsey Times* in Guernsey County, Ohio. This was discerned from the opening sentence of the article that mentions a column known to have been published in that paper. And by knowing when "Pappy Williams" lived, one can narrow down the years. The clipping does give some idea concerning the quaintness and pastoral setting of the cottage.

Newspapers. We have already mentioned the importance of newspaper clippings as a research tool. Entire newspapers and broadsides contain much valuable information about plants, nurseries (advertisements), garden tools, and descriptions of gardens.

Periodicals are also useful in this regard. Papers like *Harper's Weekly* and *Gleason's Pictorial*, to name but two, presented much data about landscapes and often contained sketches as illustrations.

Account Books. Account books are useful not only in showing how much particular items cost but also in indicating what items were purchased and when they were purchased. From this information we may assume, in the case of plants, the date of planting. We may also discern from this source how large the gardens might have been and what type they were, based on the number of people employed to tend them and the kinds of seeds and plants purchased and grown. It is possible to reconstruct considerable information about gardens and their details (curbing, benches, sculpture, structures) from records in account books.

Catalogues. Seed and nursery catalogues started appearing in the late colonial period and continued to improve in size and scope throughout the nineteenth century. The earliest catalogues were mainly listings of seeds and plants, but later catalogues contained drawings and sketches as well as pictures. Much valuable cultural information may be derived from these sources as well as styles and trends in plants.

Other catalogues, those selling garden furniture and furnishings, are also useful in presenting ideas as to the most popular styles of the era in question. These catalogues are hard to locate, but some have been reissued in recent years as collectors' items.

Probate Records. In dealing with residences, probate records may be a valuable descriptive resource, especially those that contain probate inventories. These inventories vary as to their degree of completeness, but during certain periods (particularly from about 1790 to 1830) they were unusually complete in some regions. We know of one instance where the varieties of fruit trees planted in an orchard are named, as well as the stepping-stones in the garden. Sometimes general plans of the grounds are included, but this is quite rare. Probate records can give you an idea of the relative wealth of the property owner, which may be useful in determining the type of garden he may have had.

Land Records. Land records or deeds quite often contain a description of a property or at least mention elements that are reference points along a boundary, such as "the SW corner of the garden wall." Trees were also used as reference points. One is more apt to find simple plans affixed to a deed than to a will or probate inventory. These plans, though general, often show buildings that are no longer extant, well locations, driveways and roads, and the locations of fields and yards. Land records are the best source in tracing ownership of a piece of property and the length of tenure for each owner.

Archaeological Investigations

Archeological digs are very useful as a research tool, and much data may be derived from them. It is exceedingly important to conduct such investigations through a professional because much damage can be done and valuable data lost through improper technique. There are particular schemes for conducting digs so as to yield maximum information with a minimum of digging. Only professionals or amateurs who have studied under such professionals possess the proper know-how.

98   Digs are especially important where very few site details remain and where little other data are available. For example, if you are unsuccessful in finding graphic or written material, a dig may be your only answer for coming up with reliable information on which to base planning decisions.

Because digs are time-consuming, they are costly. A professional can advise you as to the best way to get the job done. Oftentimes, digs make good thesis and dissertation topics for graduate students at a nearby college or university. Or, there may be an amateur group that has access to experts through their society or association. They may choose to use your site as a demonstration area. In most cases, however, you will have to rely upon benefactors or grants to finance digs.

Superficial investigation or removing just a scraping of topsoil, no deeper than two or three inches, can be conducted by amateurs. Previously we mentioned how such a practice revealed a drip line of cobblestones around a house we were studying. On that same site, similar investigation revealed a stone step that other evidence showed was at the entrance to the privy. In another location, a large leaching stone (a stone on which to place an ash barrel

Fig. 88. *Superficial site probing revealed this pit of stones, which verified hearsay stating that there were holes in the ground, lined with stones and covered with straw and other stones, for storing cabbages.*

for collecting lye for soap making) was found.

Superficial digs often yield plant material that has been lying dormant for many years. When perennial plants are submerged by decaying leaves and grass, they are often so suffocated that their root systems just barely survive. Seeds do likewise. The removal of some soil from the surface allows light, air, and beneficial gases to reach the roots and seeds, and they spring back to life.

Hearsay

Hearsay, or conversations with elderly citizens or with people who have talked with elderly citizens, can yield valuable information and leads for future research. It is not always the most reliable source of information, but sometimes it is the best available and can offer leads to other sources.

In other cases, it may be the only information you will ever obtain on a particular subject or site, so as long as you record your source as "hearsay," there is nothing wrong in using it to develop your plan. For example, on one property with which we had contact, a small walled-in plot was always referred to as "the press yard" or the place where apples were pressed to obtain the juice for cider. No written or graphic source yielded any information about a press yard. But if you have ever experienced the flies and bees that swarm around such an operation, it is quite logical to assume that a special enclosure might be set aside so that pigs might then be enclosed in the yard to eat the residue. There is no reason to believe that this was not the use of the enclosed space.

Locations for Research Sources

References may be found in any of three general locations:

1. *Local sources.* Photographic, manuscript, map, and book sections of local libraries; collections of genealogical, historical, and patriotic societies; collections of art galleries and

museums; private collections; town and county records.

2. *State and regional sources.* Photographic, manuscript, map, and book sections of county and state libraries; collections of state genealogical, historical, and patriotic societies; state and county museums and art galleries; county and state records.

3. *National sources.* Photographic, manuscript, map, book, and special collections in national libraries such as the Library of Congress; national genealogical societies; national historical groups; national art galleries and museums; national patriotic and fraternal organizations.

Developing a Philosophy and Developing a Plan

Once your site has been carefully analyzed and you have thoroughly researched and exhausted all sources of possible information, you are ready to pull all of this data together in the form of a development or restoration plan. But before you can do this, there are a few decisions that must be made.

Which period or periods will your restoration represent? There is no way to plan a restoration effectively until you have answered this question. Will your restoration bring the whole project back to the date of original construction, or will it represent a subsequent period? Or will a portion of the landscape setting represent the earliest possible period and another portion a later period?

Your research data should help you in making these decisions. Perhaps in the course of your research you discovered that a particular individual inhabited the dwelling in question for a long period of time. You may decide to represent that person's tenure. Or another individual, representing a different or particularly interesting profession, may be the subject of your restoration. Or you may conclude that the building should represent all the periods

100 through which it passed and that the landscape should follow this theme. Your decision
must be made on the basis of careful thinking
based on extensive research. Also, what pres-
ently exists on the site should be a deciding
factor. For example, if most of your buildings
are nineteenth century and the dwelling is late
eighteenth century, it seems a shame to tear
the outbuildings down and construct new
eighteenth century types with their corres-
ponding landscapes.

You may choose to make your restoration
conform to other restorations in the region, or
on the other hand, you may wish to contrast
with them. In New England, for example,
there are so many eighteenth century buildings open to the public and so few nineteenth
century structures that individuals who can
conveniently do so should offer a nineteenth
century setting to round out the offering in
that region.

Houses and the grounds that surround them
dominate the restoration scene. We should do
more restorative work in the areas of farms,
industrial sites, and commercial settings as
well as in the social areas such as schools,
libraries, and town centers. Landscape settings
around these types of structures may not be as
appealing to research and restore, but they are
an important part of our historical past.

Developing the Plan

Once you have gathered site and landscape
data, the next step is to develop the plan for
restoring the grounds surrounding the building or buildings in question. It is wise to select
a competent accredited and registered landscape architect for this project. The landscape
architect should be one who specializes in
historic landscapes.

In making this selection you must distin-
guish between a landscape architect who
specializes in historic preservation and one
who specializes in historic landscapes. The
two are not the same. Professionals dealing in

the former are more concerned with designing
landscapes for downtowns where old buildings are preserved and for creating a setting
for them. They become involved with adaptive
uses to meet present-day needs and problems.
Professionals who deal with the latter are
experts in period design and the interpretation
of research for a particular era. They have the
ability to think in the style of the period you
select and to have a clear understanding of
what landscapes were like at that time.

The best way to select a landscape architect
for your project is to ask to see what work he
or she has done in period design. Landscape
architects expect to present a compendium of
their works, so you will not be demanding
anything out of the ordinary. You should
interview several of them and barrage them
with all kinds of questions designed to determine their capabilities in the realm of period
design.

You may even wish to conduct a competi-
tion in which you set up guidelines and ask
for the submission of conceptual plans for the
project. If you do this, you will have to make
your research findings available for all contes-
tants. From this common base, plans will be
developed and submitted. Based on a careful
study of these, you will award your commis-
sion, and the landscape architect will then
develop the detailed final plans.

When you select a landscape architect, it is
wise, if possible, to select one who resides and
practices not too distantly from the site. This is
not always possible to accomplish because
landscape architects who specialize in historic
landscapes are limited. But if it is possible for
you to select one from close by, it will save you
money in travel fares and travel time, and he
will have a better knowledge of soil conditions, weather factors, and plant materials
adapted to your region.

The landscape architect you select should
not be so involved in historic landscapes that
he loses sight of modern needs such as circula-

tion, parking, and related problems. While it is important to present an authentically correct restoration, we do have to face the fact that the site is open to tourists, and they must be handled carefully and efficiently and in a manner that causes the least amount of wear and tear on the site.

Handling Modern Circulation Problems

When you are planning your restored landscape, it is not enough to think entirely of the authenticity of the project or making the site historically correct. Superimposed upon that important goal is another—that of making the site easily accessible and usable by those who will visit. A site that does not have an adequate circulation system will suffer much wear, tear, and abuse.

To begin with, your restored site must be properly identified so that visitors can easily find it and know when they have arrived at the site. A simple but effective sign, properly set off by background plantings will usually accomplish this goal. By simple we mean a sign with a minimum amount of lettering and also a minimum amount of ornamentation. There should be no more than twelve syllables on your sign, and its outline should be plain and uninvolved. Its standard should also be simple and in scale with the lettered portion of the sign.

Near the entrance there should be a drop-off area large enough to accommodate traffic. This drop-off area should not be for parking but rather should be a place where automobile or bus drivers can stop to allow passengers to dismount. Vehicles must then proceed to a parking area. The drop-off space should be separated from the main traffic flow by a traffic island, which can be attractively planted with low shrubs or flowers so as not to obstruct visibility. (See figures 90, 91.)

If the site you are restoring is immediately adjacent to a parking lot or if access to the site from the parking lot is close and direct, then a

Fig. 89. *A simple sign. It is unornamented and contains just the most essential information. Its edges are simple and crisp. It does not clutter or confuse.*

drop-off spot is not necessary. But if the parking lot is some distance away, such as several hundred feet or across a major thoroughfare, then it is wise to have a drop-off place for the safety and convenience of your visitors. If you only have a dozen or so visitors each day, you may not be able to justify the construction of a drop-off area.

Information and ticket centers are generally located near the entrance of the site or within one of the primary buildings on the site. If the entrance approach is long, it is wise to have the ticket-information booth near its beginning. Visitors often resent having to travel some distance by foot only to find that the admission fee is too steep or that it is not the type of site they wanted to visit.

Ticket-information centers should be de-

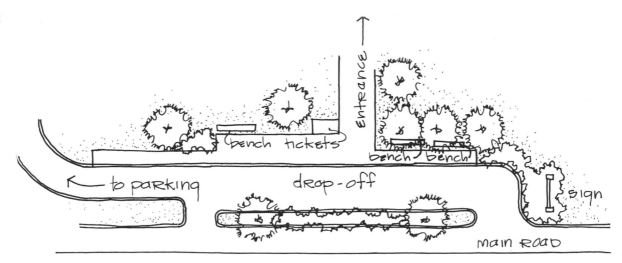

Fig. 90. *A drop-off area that is separated from the main stream of traffic. This arrangement adds an element of safety to the total plan.*

signed so that they are not an obstruction to the normal flow of traffic, unless of course you are using them as a gate. In either case, the booth should be so sited that out-going traffic is not obstructed by in-going traffic. Also, there should be sitting space somewhere near the booth so that handicapped, elderly, or tired individuals can sit while tickets are being purchased.

The whole unit (ticket-information booth and benches) should be set in an appropriate landscape of lawn or pavement with attractive plantings to soften and tie the whole together. When the area is small, it is ridiculous to have narrow walks connecting the booth and bench or rest areas. Instead, the entire space might be paved with a suitable material. If narrow walks and lawn are used, visitors will soon tread the lawn to mud, creating an unsightly as well as untidy situation.

If the site is complex, meaning that there are many parts of buildings in the area, a map can be most useful to the visitors. The map should be carefully drawn so that it is a simple but

accurate representation of what is within. The map should be placed close to the sitting or resting place so that it can be studied before the purchase of tickets. If properly drawn and graphically represented, it will help to sell admission tickets. Visitors might also be handed a printed map to use while touring the site.

Circulation within the site should be continuous, easy, and free flowing. While it is important to follow an authentic plan, we must also acknowledge the natural desire lines of traffic flow and realize that these will be followed whether we like it or not unless we provide rigid controls. All this means that people do not turn corners by making a right angle. Instead, they turn corners short, in the form of a quarter circle. It behooves us, then, to design our walk system so that corners are rounded or so that barriers are constructed to prevent this rounding out. Too many barriers, however, can visually deteriorate a site.

We recently were involved in the layout of a historic site where three buildings were

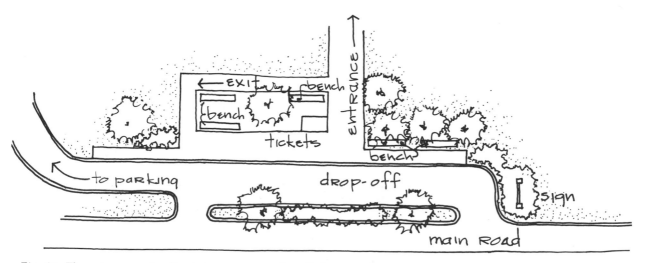

Fig. 91. *The entrance and exit points are separated to eliminate confusion. This is merely a basic concept that can be adapted to a variety of local site situations.*

planned around a central green lawn. A walk was designed along the outer edges of this grass panel. Instead of laying out the walk so that its corners were squared off, we rounded the intersections knowing that visitors would do so anyway. We could have constructed low barriers, but because the space was relatively small, we did not wish to introduce unnecessary elements which would clutter the space.

In designing circulation systems, be sure to make the walks wide enough to handle the traffic. Primary walks, those leading onto and off the site or those connecting major portions of the site, must be wide enough to handle the traffic. For moderate crowds this means that they should be at least six feet wide. For very large crowds, walks twelve to fifteen feet wide are better. Secondary or tertiary walks, such as those within a garden, can be narrower. These walks can be as narrow as three feet, and if the space is not traveled through very much, two-foot walks can also be used.

Again, it is important to make walks wide enough to handle traffic. If you don't, much site destruction will result. As a site deterior-

ates visually, it demands less respect from the visitors and still more damage will be done. It is difficult to decide how much to give in to modern circulation problems and still be able to preserve authenticity. It is our belief that the plan and the general design of the site should be rigidly authentic, but when a decision is made to allow tourists to enter, they have to be accommodated in such a way that they can use the site without abusing it.

One way to eliminate circulation problems is to avoid dead-end walks. For example, if a garden path comes to a dead end, a bottleneck will be created with consequent destruction to the garden itself. Circulation must be free flowing if the site is to work well. Actually, in history, few gardens were designed with dead-end walks because they were always a maintenance problem for the gardener, so there is little precedent for them.

Respectful tourists are happy tourists, and one thing that makes tourists happy is a place to rest or a way to move at their own pace. Elderly and handicapped people tend to move more slowly than younger people. Visitors

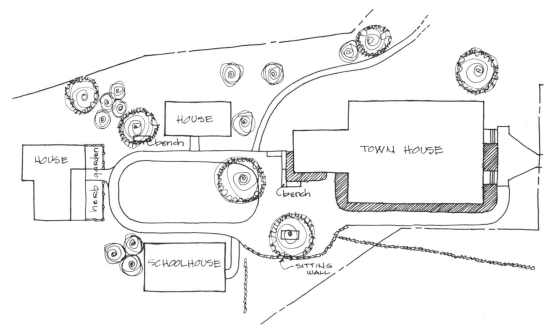

Fig. 92. This circulation scheme recognizes that people are not robots and hence do not naturally turn corners by making right angles. Note how the walk angles are curved.

who are intensely interested in the site and wish to study it also move slowly. Your circulation plan should provide places where visitors can remove themselves from the main path to rest, to talk, or to read a long label or description. These are called eddying places, and your plan should provide them.

Benches should be placed in spots that are pleasant, such as where there is a view, vista, or some shade. It is also a good idea to place them after a steep climb or an otherwise strenuous part of the site. These sitting places should be removed from the mainstream of traffic so that they do not obstruct normal flow. People like to stop to read or reflect without having pedestrians trip over their feet.

If your site is interpreted by a docent, there should be eddying spots in the landscape so that groups can stop for instruction without interfering with others who are not being taught. It is very distracting to both the student-visitors and pedestrians to be interrupted by one another.

Parking lots cost much money to construct, and they are often ugly to look at. If you are fortunate enough to be located near a school or church or some other type of site that does not use its parking lot much during the summer, you may be able to work out an arrangement whereby you allow your visitors to park in your neighbor's parking lot. Unfortunately, this kind of arrangement can only be worked out in a few cases.

If you must construct your own parking area, locate it so that it is outside the authentic portion of your site and carefully screened from it. There is nothing that will destroy the mood and motif of your site more than a series of parked cars or even a single one for that matter. For this reason, large buffer zones

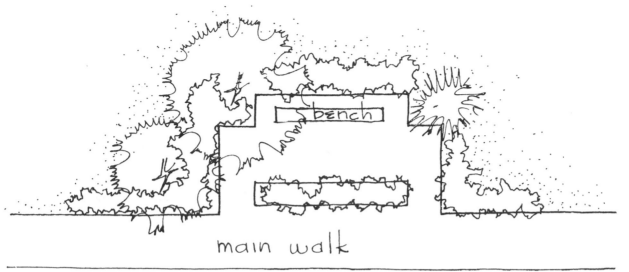

Fig. 93. *An eddying spot where people or a single person can retire from the mainstream of traffic to rest or study the site. This basic scheme may be adapted to suit local conditions.*

consisting of hedges or shrubbery are important. Hedges should be wide enough to do the job adequately, at least four feet. Shrub borders should be at least twelve to fifteen feet wide.

If your parking lot accommodates more than twenty-five cars, it is a good idea to plant some trees on islands within the lot. These trees should not be mathematically placed so that after every twenty-five cars there is a tree. It is better to cluster them here and there so that the lot is visually broken up in an interesting way.

In some instances, it may be easier to break your lot up into a few small lots. This utilizes more land than having the parking area in one block, but it may be the best way to design the lot if flat areas are at a minimum. Less site destruction occurs in this way, and the parking fits better into the site. The lawn areas between can be generously planted with trees and shrubs.

The walkway leading from the parking lot to the main circulation system through the site should be clearly visible and treated so that it is safe. It should not be obscure or located so that one must walk between cars to reach it. It should be accented with plantings or architectural features so that it stands out as an entrance place.

Safety is of utmost importance in solving modern circulation problems. Junctures of foot traffic with vehicular traffic should be clearly marked and visually unobstructed. The pavement used in walkways must be safe underfoot. If the site is used at night, lighting should be installed for the visitors' protection as well as for protection against vandalism. In primary circulation systems, steps should be avoided whenever possible. Steps may be used within secondary systems, such as in a garden.

The Restoration Plan

Most plans for garden restorations and re-creations include a prescribed set of directions shown in plan view and through construction details. In addition, a written set of specifica-

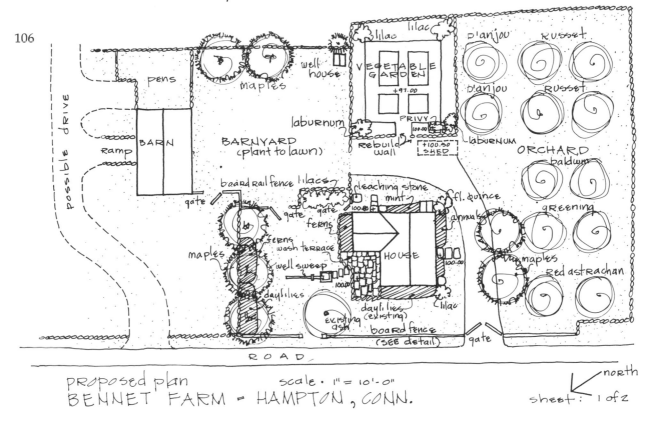

The following labels appear on the plan:

possible drive · pens · well house · lilac · lilac · d'anjou · russet · maples · VEGETABLE GARDEN +97.00 · d'anjou · russet · BARN · ramp · Ramp · BARNYARD (plant to lawn) · laburnum · PRIVY 100.00 · laburnum · ORCHARD baldwin · gate · board rail fence lilacs · Rebuild Wall · +100.30 SHED · greening · ferns · gate · gate · bleaching stone · mint · fl. quince · annuals · maples · ferns · wash terrace · HOUSE · 100.00 · Red astrachan · well sweep · 100.00 · daylilies · existing ash · daylilies (existing) · lilac · board fence (SEE detail) · gate · ROAD

PROPOSED plan scale · 1" = 10'-0" north
BENNET FARM – HAMPTON, CONN. sheet: 1 of 2

Fig. 94-A. *A finished landscape plan, with plant specifications and construction details shown in figure 94-B. Note the various details mentioned in the text.*

tions are included to cover all items that cannot be shown on the plan. Plans for such projects include the following:

1. The placement and location of all features of the plan, including buildings, circulation systems, walls, fences, garden features, and any other elements that should appear in the executed plan.

2. Construction details for all these features. These details must include precise measurements and a list of materials. (See figure 94-B.)

3. The location for all plants and specifications for plant sizes. Specifications must include botanical as well as common names. The quantities of each plant are listed as well as any other particular aspect about each plant.

For example, if a lilac is to be a clump rather than a single stem, this should be indicated.

4. Grass or lawn seed should be specified in the specifications. The percentage of each species that will compose the mixture should be stated as well as the rate of application.

5. All existing and proposed contours and building elevations. Also spot elevations for steps, drains, and culverts.

6. If the work is not to be completed all at once, it should be indicated on the plan which portion shall be phase one, two, three, etc.

In conducting restoration work, you must provide detailed plans to go out for bids so that the bidder will know what he is bidding on and the owner will be sure what he will

PLANT SPECIFICATIONS

QUANTITY	NAME	SIZE
	APPLES (MALUS)	3'-4'
4	RUSSET	
2	BALDWIN	
2	GREENING	
2	RED ASTRACHAN	
1	FLOWERING QUINCE. CHAENOMELES LAGENARIA	2'
2	LABURNUM ANAGYROIDES	4'-6'
3	LILAC - SYRINGA VULGARIS	4'-6'
10	MINT - MENTHA SPICATA	1 YR.
10	MAPLES (SUGAR) - ACER SACCHURUM	3" CAL.
3	PEAR - D'ANJOU - PYRUS COMMUNIS	3'-4'
1	PINE (WHITE) - PINUS STROBUS	4'-6'

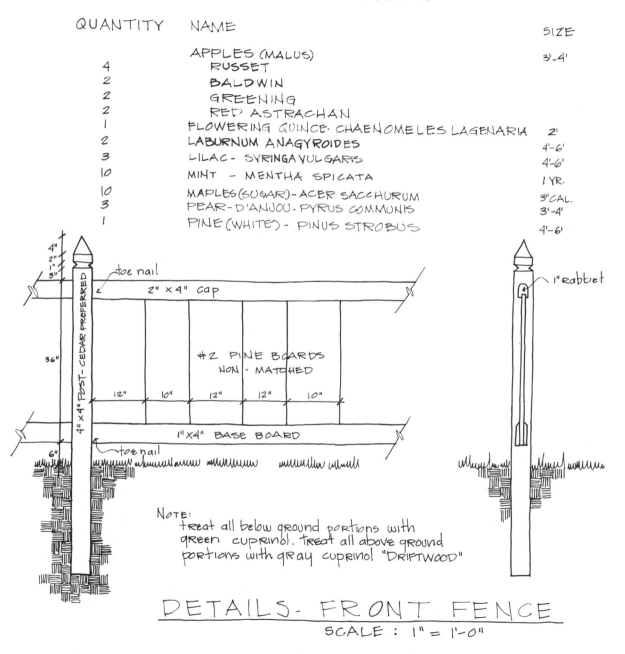

4"
2"
1"
3"
toe nail
2" x 4" cap
4" x 4" POST - CEDAR PREFERRED
36"
#2 PINE BOARDS
NON - MATCHED
12" 10" 12" 12" 10"
1" X 4" BASE BOARD
toe nail
6"

1" rabbet

NOTE:
treat all below ground portions with green cuprinol. treat all above ground portions with gray cuprinol "DRIFTWOOD"

DETAILS - FRONT FENCE
SCALE : 1" = 1'-0"

Fig. 94-B. *Plant specifications and construction details for finished landscape plan shown in figure 94-A.*

108 receive for the work performed. In other words, the more precise the plans and specifications are, the more precise the bids will be as well as the work when it is performed. Yet, in many cases, it is desirable not to draw precise plans so that the finished work will appear less stiff and contrived. An example of this is an informal dooryard garden. The designer may wish to show the fence design as well as the layout for the paths and the materials to be used in paving them. But, in order to achieve a quaint effect, the precise location for each plant should be decided as they are planted.

To achieve this effect, then, the designer should merely provide a list of the plants to be planted with a note on the plan that the designer will be on site to supervise the planting. This approach takes co-ordination between the designer, the owner, and the contractor performing the work. The resulting effect, though, is 100 percent better because the plants can be installed as they are taken from the truck as opposed to working from a plan where the layout was thought out on a drafting table.

This approach to landscape restoration is not new. The English have used it for years. After thoroughly researching the site as well as the written and graphic records, they make general decisions as to the proposed restoration. Plans are drawn reflecting general ideas and concepts. Then work proceeds and "as built" plans are drawn for the historical record. In so doing, the resultant project looks quite real, and modifications that must be made as work progresses are reflected on the final plan.

Interpretive Markers

While a restored site should function well with a minimum of direction signs, some interpretive signs are needed to explain historical facts or to identify parts of the restoration. There are many kinds of interpretive signs, but we feel that those that create the least amount of visual intrusion to the site are the most desirable.

Interpretive signs should be quite low to the ground and not above waist level. In fact, signs that are about two feet from the ground are ideal because they intrude less on the overall site. Children are able to see them as well as adults. When signs are waist high or higher, they destroy the overall landscape effect and attract all of the attention to themselves.

We feel that there should be a minimum of signs, not only because they destroy the visual appearance of the site but also because they are expensive to purchase and to maintain. They are also attractive to vandals and souvenir seekers. Only points of utmost importance should be marked. Other points should be described in a brochure to be read by the visitor.

When possible, it is desirable to affix signs to buildings or fences or other existing free-standing elements. In this way, it is not necessary to install additional freestanding obstructions to the site. But in this case, too, only major points should be identified and other points should be covered in a brochure.

Plants are often labeled on small labels, about two inches by three inches, on a wire stand. In some cases, it may be necessary to label individual plants, but overlabeling tends to destroy the overall effect of a garden. We prefer mounting a plan showing the name and location of each plant in a central place in the garden and also including the plan in the brochure. The garden then stands as a garden rather than a "botanical collection."

There are disadvantages to both sides of this picture. People read signs more than brochures, but they are costly and obtrusive. Brochures are not cheap, either. Many people do not read them and some litter the premises with them. A system whereby visitors are not forced to accept a brochure but can receive one if they desire seems best.

3

*Authentic Plants for Period
Landscape Settings*

$\mathcal{T}$HE major purpose of this section is to provide you with an extensive list of authentic plants for restoration work and to discuss styles and trends in the use and availability of plant material throughout the various periods.

Trends and Styles

It has already been mentioned in this text that during the colonial period, nurseries and seed houses were very few. The most important ones and their founding dates were as follows:

John Bartram, Philadelphia, 1728
Robert Prince, Flushing, Long Island, 1735
Joseph Cooper, Gloucester County, N.J., 1746
Henry Laurens, Anson Borough, S.C., c. 1750
John Watson, Charleston, S.C., 1763
David Landreth, Philadelphia, 1784
Robert Squib, Charleston, S.C., 1785

Before the advent of nurseries and seed houses, plants were introduced to this country by the immigrants. Plants were distributed among passengers on board ships. Many plants were exchanged from housewife to housewife and from farmer to farmer. These plant and seed exchanges perpetuated the same few varieties or even inferior crosses that had resulted through cross-pollination and self-seeding in dooryard gardens. As a result, the plants of the colonial period were simple in appearance, meaning that plants with exotic leaves and flowers were not sought after. Most plants were grown for their fragrance and culinary and medicinal use. Appearance was bottom on the list of plant preferences.

Few evergreens were planted in colonial landscapes, and those that were consisted of native species, such as cedars, pines, and arborvitaes. Boxwood and inkberry were two exceptions. Because evergreens were not popular, the landscape appeared quite dismal and austere in winter.

The planting of ornamental trees did not gain general favor until after the colonial period. Trees used for shade tended to be native trees left as land was cleared or indigenous species gathered from the woods and forests. There was more interest in clearing land than in planting trees. When trees were planted, the list consisted of apples, pears, peaches, cherries, and any other fruit tree that would grow and provide much-needed delicacies. Fruit trees were a very major part of the American landscape throughout the seventeenth and eighteenth centuries.

On the ornamental side, bulbs and roses have always been popular American flowers, starting with the earliest settlements and extending to the present gardens. Daffodils, crocuses, scillas, and many other bulbs, corms, and tubers were very early introduced into Europe and brought here by the colonists. Roses, such as Sweetbriers, Province, and Moss, were favorites in ancient gardens mainly for their fragrance. While types and varieties of these plants have changed, these genera have always headed the list for American gardens.

Herbs of all kinds and uses have always had major standing in American gardens. In recent years, herbs have been grown largely for appearance, but in earlier times they were essential for food, medicine, and as masking for foul odors. Most herbs were dried so that they could be used in the winter months as well as during the growing season, meaning that the plants from which they were cut didn't always look their best in the garden. But it really didn't matter because herbs were usually grown in combination with other plants.

As we became a new nation, our grounds gradually changed in general appearance. More attention was paid to the use of trees. Ornamental species were being introduced

Fig. 95. *The house of Bishop Benjamin Moore, in New York, called The Pulpit. Fastigiate and weeping plants, or any plant with exaggerated form, became popular in the Victorian period.*

through the nursery trade and through commerce around the world. Many estate owners planted groves on their properties. Thomas Jefferson was one who established a grove of at least eighteen acres on Monticello mountain, his principal home, near Charlottesville, Virginia.

The nursery and seed trade began to swell to large proportions. The following establishments were founded between 1785 and 1850:

James Bloodgood, Flushing, N.Y., 1798
John Gardiner and David Hepburn, Washington, D.C., c. 1800
Bernard McMahon, Philadelphia, 1804
Grant Thorburn, N.Y., N.Y., 1805
Charles Downing, Newburgh, N.Y., c. 1810
John Adlum, near Washington, D.C., 1814
J. H. Stark, Louisiana, Mo., 1816

Joseph Breck, Boston, Mass., 1818
Thomas Hogg, New York, N.Y., 1822
William Kenrick, Newton, Mass., 1823
Robert Manning, Salem, Mass. 1823
Andre Paremtier, Brooklyn, N.Y., 1825
Nicholas Longworth, Cincinnati, Ohio, 1828
Thomas Hibbert and Robert Buist, Philadelphia, 1830
Samuel Feast, Baltimore, Md., c. 1830
Thomas Bridgeman, New York, N.Y., c. 1830
Charles Hovey, Cambridge, Mass., 1834
Samuel B. Parsons, Flushing, N.Y., 1838
Henry A. Dreer, Philadelphia, 1838
George Ellanger and Patrick Barry, Rochester, N.Y., 1840
Peter Henderson, Jersey City, N.J., 1847
Douglas Robert, Waukegan, Ill., 1848
Many of these horticulturists also authored

books on gardening and landscaping that were very helpful to those wishing to lay out their grounds in the latest style.

Because of the numerous **nursery** and seeds tradesmen, plants of many species became readily available to those who wished to purchase them, working hand in hand with the latest concept of mixed tree and shrub plantings to separate various parts of the grounds and to accentuate the boundaries. The list at the end of this section shows that many more evergreens were used. Designers, such as Downing, called for them in their plans to achieve the "picturesque." Even the list of perennial plants shows a greater variety of material and a tendency toward more colorful and exotic plants.

Street trees were being installed throughout the nation. Suddenly there was great interest in lining roads and streets with trees. Towns organized committees to reach these goals. In 1802, the town of Canton, Massachusetts, formed a committee to procure Lombardy **poplars** (a popular tree of that period) and "place them in such order around the meeting house as shall tend to ornament and convenience." Many other towns also planted their main buildings and streets in a similar manner.

In this early part of the nineteenth century, vines also became popular. They were planted on trellises or just on a dead tree stump. Vine-covered summerhouses or rustic seats or vine-covered outbuildings were an important part of the landscape and a trend toward the emerging "gardenesque" style. Trellis arches were placed at entrances to gardens or around the main door of the house. If the vines were not severely pruned, they tended to overcome their support and run "wild" over the trellis or building, hence the image of the "vine-covered cottage."

During the second half of the nineteenth century, or the Victorian period, nurseries and seed houses were founded at an **even greater**

rate than previously. Plant explorations were organized and conducted, bringing a wide array of new, different, and exotic material to our land. As mentioned in the first part of this book, the Victorian era was a time when horticulture was golden. Daring combinations of plants were brought together in the form of flower and carpet beds. Hothouses, to grow every kind of tropical plant available, were

Fig. 96. *Vines became more popular than ever before in the late nineteenth century. Because they need support, various kinds of trellis designs emerged, ranging from wood to wire as shown here.*

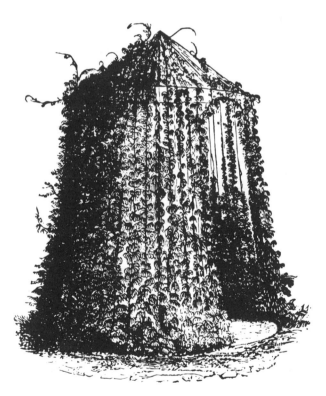

Fig. 97. *Simple trellises consisted of nothing more than a dead cedar trunk inserted into the ground.*

Fig. 98. *Some vine supports were simply strings tied to a central pole or a more complex arrangement such as this "pavilion."*

Fig. 99. *Bedding plants, arranged in a ribbon design, and mounded in the center. The mounds were usually accentuated with bold plants. Agaves were popular for this use, as were certain grasses.*

116 built by those that could afford them.

Plants with definite forms, possessing bold lines and texture, were planted throughout grounds to complement similar boldness and exaggerated form in architecture. Large tufts of ornamental grasses accentuated gardens and landscapes. Large weeping specimen trees were set in vast lawns. Weeping plants, such as beeches, cherries, and mulberries, were extremely popular. But that form was not exclusively for trees. Garden flowers, such as weeping amaranth or love-lies-bleeding, were also planted.

Plants with bold leaves, like coltsfoot and gunnera, were employed as accents in the landscape. Peonies, which had been popular even during earlier times, were combined in large masses collectively to add boldness of texture and form. The plant list at the end of this section contains numerous plants with bold and exotic form and texture for the period from 1850 to 1900.

In the late nineteenth century, certain plants became less popular. These were plants that had been grown "since the beginning." Such flowers as perennial sunflowers, daylilies, poppies, biennial hollyhocks, larkspurs, pansies, stock, nasturtiums, and seathrift were considered too "old-fashioned" or flowers for "grandmother's garden." Some who liked these "quaint" plants continued to grow them and purposely created "grandmother's gardens," but they were not in the majority.

Procuring Period Plants

Finding the species given in the list that follows is not difficult, but finding old varieties of these species is quite a chore. This is because plant breeders and hybridizers have developed newer varieties; as soon as new ones are developed, the older ones are rejected. Consequently, if you wish to grow the very old varieties of plants for your garden, for purposes of authenticity, you will have a difficult time.

For example, hyacinths that we purchase today are strong, erect, and clubby. Older varieties were loose growing, with flowers far apart on the stalk. It is virtually impossible to purchase these. Or try to purchase seeds of simple white, pink, or purple petunias that are not hybrids. That is also very difficult.

Further on we present a list of plant sources. While all these nurseries and seed houses do not specialize in authentic varieties, it is possible to purchase from some of them var-

Fig. 100. *Grasses, such as this clump of pampas, were either planted in the center of beds or incorporated into flower borders. Sometimes they were set directly into the lawn.*

Fig. 101. *Strict and erect plant forms, such as this false cypress, were planted as accents in the landscape. Specifically, they were used to enframe entrances to gardens, as sculptural elements, and as foundation plantings during the late nineteenth century.*

Fig. 102. *Stately trees were an important part of nineteenth-century landscapes, planted either singly or in groups.*

Fig. 103. *Weeping plants are another example of the exaggerated forms used in Victorian landscapes. They were most often grown as single specimens, such as this weeping beech.*

Fig. 104. *Landscape showing a combination of several plant forms in a manner typical of the Victorian period.*

120

Fig. 105. *Bold-foliaged plants were extremely popular in the Victorian period and were planted in exotic combinations. The tallest plants are castor beans. They are surrounded by cannas, caladiums, coleus, and centaureas.*

ieties of flowers that are close to the original species.

It is a good idea to maintain a small nursery where you can collect authentic plants from individuals and also where you can allow plants to revert. For example, going back to hyacinths, if you let a row of them grow in a small nursery without resetting them from time to time, they will get loose and sparse and quite like the old varieties. And if you let many annuals go to seed and then collect the

seeds and plant them, the seedlings will revert. Eventually, through this process, you will obtain plants that are similar to old varieties.

It is wise through publicity and campaigns to get word around that you are looking for old varieties of trees, shrubs, and perennials. We have done this for many projects with great success. The following is a description of one iris that was sent to us as a result of such an effort:

BLUE FLAG

In one of the first letters that Mary Willemsen Gardiner, wife of Lion Gardiner, wrote home to Holland, she said, "The blue flags that we brought with us are doing nicely in our kitchen garden." The kitchen garden, with a large bed of blue flags, was perpetuated by the proprietors of Gardiner's Island until Clarence MacKay took over a lease on the Manor House as well as the shooting preserve. He tore out the kitchen garden to make an automobile entrance to the Manor House for his bride, Anna Case, the Metropolitan opera singer.

In 1912 my father (G. Duane Cooper), my uncle, A. Gardiner Cooper, and I visited Gardiner's Island. Lion Gardiner welcomed us cordially. When we were leaving, he asked if I would like a piece of the island for myself, but I replied that I already had some stones from the island in my pocket. He said that he had in mind something living since the island's earliest days, and he himself dug a clump of blue flags and told me their history.

I divided the clump between our yard at Shelton Island Heights and the Cooper-Gardiner plot in the Sag Harbour Cemetery, where they bloomed again last spring, 1952.

My clump at Shelton Island has flourished and multiplied so that I have given clumps from it to Sylvester Manor on Shelton Island, to Miss Sarah Gardiner in East Hampton, and the President's house at Yale.

In 1949 I relocated my clump at Shelton Island Heights, where it has not done well, so I will relocate it again next week.

(Signed)   Starr Gardiner Cooper

Fig. 106. *Gunneras were very much sought after as bold-foliaged plants.*

Fig. 107. *A typical "grandmother's garden," quaint in appearance.*

122 The iris, when received, was planted and allowed to flower. It is quite unlike any modern variety and quite resembles ancient drawings and paintings of blue flag.

List of Sources

No list of sources can ever be complete. Nevertheless, we present this one, which we have used extensively, as a beginning. No one of these nurseries or seed houses will offer every plant you seek. You will have to research them all, against your specified list, and purchase some plants from one and some from another.

Seeds

Conn.	Comstock-Ferre Seed Co., Wethersfield
Ill.	R. H. Shumway, Seedsman, 628 Cedar St., Rockford
Iowa	Field Seed & Nursery Co., Shenandoah
Minn.	Farmer Seed & Nursery Co., Faribault
N.J.	Thompson & Norctan, Box 24, Kennedy Blvd., Somerdale (also Ipswich, England)
N.Y.	Herbst Brothers Seedsmen, Inc., 678 Broadway, N.Y.
Pa.	Burpee Seeds, Warminster
S.C.	George Park Seed Co., Greenwood

Plants

Calif.	Will Tillotson Roses, Watsonville
Conn.	Bristol Nurseries, Inc., Pinehurst Road, Bristol
	Caprilands Herb Farm, Coventry
	Millane Nurseries & Tree Experts, Inc., Cromwell
	White Flower Farm, Litchfield
England	Sutton Seeds, Reading
Ga.	Cedar Lane Farms, Madison
Ill.	Lounsberry Gardens, Oakford
Iowa	Inter-State Nurseries, Inc., Hamburg
Maine	Western Maine Forest Nursery Co., 36 Elm St., Fryeburg
Md.	Bluemont Nurseries, Inc., Monkton
Mass.	Weston Nursery, Hopkinton
Mich.	Ackerman Nurseries, Bridgman
	Burgess Seed & Plant Co., Galesburg
	Emlong's Nurseries, Inc., Stevensville
Mo.	Stark Bros. Nurseries & Orchards Co., Louisiana

N.J.	Eastern Roses, Box 203, West Long Branch
	Vermeulen & Son, Inc., Woodfern Rd., Neshanic Station
N.Y.	Jackson & Perkins Co., Newark
	Kelly Bros. Nurseries, Inc., 23 Maple St., Dansville
	J. E. Miller Nurseries, Canandaigua
	Stern's Nurseries, Inc., Geneva
	Martin Viette, East Norwich, Long Island
N.C.	Gardens of the Blue Ridge, Ashford, Mac-Dowell County
Ohio	Cole-American Garden, Circleville
	Rocknoll Nursery, R.R. 1, Morrow
S.C.	Wayside Gardens, Hodges
S. Dak.	Gurney's Inc., 2nd and Capitol Sts., Yankton
Tenn.	Tennessee Nursery Co., Cleveland
Vt.	Putney Nursery, Inc., Putney
Va.	Gulf Stream Nursery, Inc. Wachapreague
	Ingleside Plantation Nurseries, Oak Grove
	The Tankard Nurseries, Ocean Highway, U.S. 13, Exmore
	Watkins Nurseries, Midlothian
Wash.	Buckley Nursery Co., Buckley
	Columbia & Okanogan Nursery Co. P.O. Box 116, Wenatchee
	Malmo Whidbey Nursery Co., 6050 50th NE, Seattle
	Richmond Nurseries, Richmond Beach
	Stanek's, 2929 27th Ave., Spokane
	Taylor Nurseries, 4647 Union Bay Place, Seattle

Old Fruit Varieties [1]

Colo.	H. L. Norlin, Fort Collins
Ga.	Fruitland Nurseries, Augusta
	Kay Nurseries, Royston
	North Georgia Nursery, Cleveland
	O'Neil Hitt, Jasper
	Willoughby's Nurseries, Waco
Iowa	R. M. Clark, Mitchellville
	Mrs. Albert Kloppenborg, Newton
	Clair P. Lauer, Eldorado
	Wheelock Wilson Nursery, Marshalltown
Kans.	Warren Wakeman, Orchard House, Osawatomie
Mass.	Worcester Horticulture Society, 30 Elm St., Worcester
Mich.	M. Farley, Jr., Albion
	V. Friday, Coloma
	R. Hyde, Fenton

---

1. See Appendix.

	E. Mawby, Portland
	W. Mueller, Linden
	R. Nitschke, 2362 Tilbury Place, Birmingham
	J. Rickert, Shelby
Mo.	R. G. Anderson, 9251 Lee Blvd., Kansas City
N.H.	Ira Glackens, Center Conway
N.J.	H. W. Schroeder, Boonton
N.Y.	Fred Ashworth, Heuvelton
	R. W. Daniels, Rt. 1, Potsdam
	Richard M. Fagley, 24 Commodore Rd., Chappaqua
Ohio	Walter A. Cope, 205 E. No. Broadway, Columbus
Oreg.	Arneson Nursery Co., Canby
	Carlton Nursery Co., Forest Grove
	Milton Nursery Co., Milton
	Rich and Sons Nursery, Hillsboro
Pa.	W. E. Bates, Stevensville
	M. L. Redding, Ridgway
Wash.	The Van Well Nursery, 1000 N. Miller St., Wenatchee

An excellent reference for many other plant sources is *Nursery Source Guide*, vol. 33, no. 2 (Summer 1977), of the *Brooklyn Botanical Garden Record, Plants and Gardens*.

List of Authentic Plants for Recreating Period Landscapes

The following list of plants for period landscapes is extensive. It represents many years of research, and the list is original. This means that we developed it from sources contemporary with the periods discussed, not from lists developed by others in recent years.

We have not included the documentation for every plant listed because that would make this work too cumbersome. But within our files each plant is listed on an index card with the exact source or sources recorded.

If a plant does not appear on this list for a particular period, it does not mean that it was not grown. It simply means that we have not found it in works of that period and therefore have no documentation for it.

We have been careful not to include plants on the list for a particular period unless we are sure that they were generally used. For example, white petunias were introduced from Brazil in 1823 and purple ones from Argentina in 1830. Most plants, when introduced, take a few years to reach the seed and nursery trade. We found that petunias were not generally planted until the 1850 to 1900 period, so they are not included in our list until then. We have followed this rationale throughout.

Many of the common names for the plants listed will appear misspelled according to today's standards, but that is the way they were spelled in the period that they represent. We have purposely not modernized spellings, so that users of the list may more readily find what they are looking for in consulting early sources.

(sp = species, var. = variety, X = cross, * = plants that have been listed earlier on this list but are popular enough to be mentioned again, fl. pl. = double-flowering varieties, frequently seen in old plant lists as flora-plen, flore-pleno, flo-plen, pleni-flora, pleno, or florepleno)

FLOWERS—1600–1699

Achillea millefolium	Yarrow
Aconitum napellus	Aconitum, Wolfsbane
Althaea rosea	Hollyhock, Garden or French Mallows, "single, double & several colors"
Amaranthus caudatus	Love-lies-bleeding, Tassel Flower, Flower Gentle, "used by country women"
Amaranthus tricolor	Tri-color Amaranth or Joseph's Coat
Anemone coronaria, probably	Anemone, tuberous types
Anemone pulsatilla	Pasque Flower, Windflower or Emanies
Antirrhinum majus	Snapdragon, "red, white, purple, variable"
Aquilegia sp.	Columbine, "singles and doubles"
Asphodelus albus	Asphodell
Asphodelus luteus	Asphodell or King's Spear
Aster sp.	Aster, Starwort
Bellis perennis	English Daisy, Herb Margaret, Ewe- or May-gowan, Childing Daisy, Bone- or Bruisewort, Bone Flower, March Daisy, Bairnwort
Calendula officinalis	Calendula, "Pot Marygold"
Campanula medium	Canterbury Bells, "doubles"
Campanula persicifolia	Bellflower
Centaurea sp., probably	Centaury
Centaurea cyanus	Cornflower, Blew Bottle
Chelidonicum majus	Celandine Poppy
Chieranthus cheiri	Wallflower, "keiri"
Chrysanthemum leucanthemum, possibly or *Bellis perennis*	Daisies
Chrysanthemum parthenium	Feverfew, Fether-few
Colchicum autumnale, var. *atropurpureum*	Colchicum, Meadow Saffron
Convallaria majalis	Lily-of-the-valley
Convolvulus sp.	Convolvulus, Bindweed, Blew Bindweed, or Morning Glory, a modern name
Crocus vernus	Crocus, "white, small purple, large purple, yellow"
Cucurbita pepo var. *ovifera*, probably	Gourds
Datura stramonium	Thornapple or Jimson Weed
Delphinium ajacis	Larkspur, Delphinium or Larks Heels
Dianthus sp.	Clove, Gilliflowers or Pinks, "red and white, pink and white"
Dianthus barbatus	Sweet William, Armeria, Sweet John
Dictamnus albus	Dittany or Fraxinella
Digitalis purpurea	Foxglove

Epimedium sp., probably *alpinum* or *grandiflorum*	Epimedium or Barrenwort
Eranthis hyemalis	Winter Aconite
Eryngium maritimum	Sea Holly
Erythronium dens-canis	Dogtooth Violet, "Dens-caninus"
Fritillaria imperialis	Crown Imperial
Fritillaria meleagris	Chequered Lily
Geranium maculatum, robertianum or *lancastriense*	Cranesbill, Geranium, "blue, white, and rose"
Gladiolus sp.	Gladiolus or Corn Flag
Gomphrena globosa	Globe Amaranth, Batchelors Button
Helianthus annuus, probably	Sunflower, "very tall"
Helichrysum bracteatum	Strawflower or Everlasting
Helleborous niger	Helleborous, "the black flower at Christmas"
Hemerocallis flava	Yellow Daylily
Hemerocallis fulva	Tawny Daylily
Hepatica sp.	Hepatica, Liver-worts
Hesperis matronalis	Rocket or Dames Violet
Hyacinthus sp.	Hyacinth or Jacenths
Iberis umbellata, probably	Candytuft
Impatiens balsamina	Balsam
Innula helenium	Elecampane
Iris sp.	Iris, "flower-de-luce," "flags, blue and varied"
Iris germanica var. *florentina alba*	Iris
Iris praecox	Bulbous Iris
Iris susiana	Mourning Iris, referred to as "Turkish," bulbous
Iris variegata, could also apply to striped-leaved forms of other Irises	Iris
Iris xiphiodes	English Iris, bulbous
Lamium sp., probably *maculatum, album* or *purpureum*	Dead Nettle
Lathyrus latifolius	Perennial Sweet Pea
Leucojum vernum	Great Spring Snowdrop
Lilium auratum, L. martagon or *L. speciosum* var. *album*	White Lily
Lilium canadense	Meadow Lily
Lilium martagon	Martagon or Turks-Cap Lily
Linaria sp.	Toad Flax, Wild Flax
Lobelia cardinalis	Cardinal Flower
Lupinus sp.	Lupine
Lychnis chalcedonica	Lychnis, Maltese Cross, or Red Campion
Lychnis coronaria	Lychnis, Nonesuch, Flower of Bristow, Constantinople, Flower of Bristol
Lycopersicum esculentum	Tomato or "pomum amoris," always listed as an ornamental during this period
Mathiola incana	Gilliflower, Stock-Gilliflower or Wall-flower
Mimosa pudica	Sensitive Plant
Mirabilis jalapa	Mirabilis, Four-o'cloks, or Marvel of Peru
Monarda fistulosa	Blue Monarda
Muscari botryoides	Grape Hyacinth
Narcissus sp.	Daffodils, Daffadown Dillies, "trumpets, poets, doubles or multiplex"
Nepeta hederacea	Ground Ivy, Ale-hoof

FLOWERS—1600–1699 (Continued)

Nigella damascena	Nigella, or Fennel Flower
Ornithogallum umbellatum	Star-of-Bethlehem
Paeonia officinalis	Peony, "double red, double purple"
Papaver sp.	French Double Poppy, "ornaments of the garden," "red, scarlet, lead color, white, blush"
Parietaria officinalis	Pelletory
Physalis alkekengi	Alkekengi, Winterberry, Winter-Cherry or Chinese Lantern Plant
Primula auricula	Primroses, Cowslips, Beare's Ears, Oxslips, "purple, purple and yellow, sable, red, yellow, white"
Pulmonaria angustifolia	Lungwort
Ranunculus acris, probably	Crowsfoot, Ranunculus, Fair Maids of France, "has escaped to the wild"
Ranunculus asiatius	Garden Ranunculus, Turban or Persian
Ranunculus creticus	Creten Ranunculus
Sanguinaria canadensis	Bloodroot, Puckoon
Scabiosa atropurpurea	Scabiosa, "White and Red"
Tagetes sp.	Marygold
Tagetes erecta	African Marigold or "Flos Africanis" or "Flos Africanis Multiplex"
Tagetes patula	French Marigold—Note: While both the so-called African and French Marigolds were grown, it appears from the literature that what we know today as French Marigolds were most common. In fact, it appears that the names, African and French were used loosely to apply to *T. patula*. The issue is further confused in that Calendula (*C. officinalis*) was also called "Marygold."
Taraxacum officinale	Dandelion, Leontodon
Teucrium chamaedrys	Germander
Thalictrum aquilegifolium	Meadow Rue, Feathered Columbine
Tropaeolum majus	Nasturtium, or Indian Cress, often listed as an herb or vegetable because it was eaten (leaves and buds)
Tulipa sp.	Tulips, mainly broken types grown, also doubles and singles
Valeriana officinalis or *Polemonium caeruleum*	Valerian, Jacob's Ladder
Verbascum thapsis, probably	Verbascum, Mullein or Moth Mullein
Viola sp.	Violets
Viola tricolor	Pansy or Heart's Ease
Yucca filamentosa	Yucca

SHRUBS, TREES, AND VINES—1600–1699

Abies sp.	Fir
Acer rubrum	Red Maple
Buxus sempervirens	English Box
Campsis radicans	Trumpet Flower

Celtis occidentalis	Hackberry, American Nettle-tree
Cercis canadensis	Red-bud, Arbor-Judae, Judas Tree or Sallad Tree
Cornus amomum	Silky Dogwood
Cornus florida	Dogwood
Cornus mas	Cornelian Cherry or Cornel
Cornus stolonifera	Red Osier Dogwood
Cotinus coggygria	Smoke Tree or Venetian Sumach
Cytisus multiflorus	Spanish Cytisus, White Spanish Broom
Daphne mezereum	Mezereum, Chamelaea
Filipendula hexapetala, probably	Spirea or Dropwort—Most Spireas were not introduced until later, but the Filipendulas were called Spireas at this time.
Gelsemium sempervirens	Honeysuckle, Carolina Yellow Jessamine, Jasmine
Hamamelis virginiana	Witch Hazel
Hibiscus syriacus	Althaea, Rose-of-Sharon
Hypericum sp., possibly *Hypericum calycinum*	Hypericum, Saint John's Wort
Hypericum densiflorum	Bushy Saint John's Wort
Ilex sp.	Holly
Ilex glabra or *Ilex verticillata*, probably	Winterberry—This name sometimes refers to *Physalis alkekengi*.
Jasminum sambac	Jasmine, Arabian Pipe
Juniperus sabina	Savin Tree or Bush, Savine or Sabin Juniper
Juniperus virginiana	Juniper, Cedar, Red Cedar or Eastern Red Cedar
Laburnum anagyroides	Common Laburnum, Golden-chain or Beantree
Lantana camara	Lantana, for indoor culture
Larix decidua, probably	Larch
Ligustrum vulgare	Common Privet, Primworth, Skedge or Skedgewirth
Lindera benzoin	Spicebush
Liquidambar styracifluu	Sweet Gum
Liriodendron tulipifera	Tulip Tree
Lonicera periclymenum	Honeysuckle, French Honeysuckle, Red-Satin Flower, Woodbine, Common English Honeysuckle
Lonicera sempervirens	Scarlet, French, or Coral Honeysuckle
Magnolia virginiana	Magnolia, Sweet Bay, Swamp Magnolia or Bay Laurel
Myrica pennsylvanica	Bayberry or Wax Myrtle, Candleberry Myrtle
Parthenocissus quinquefolia	Virginia Creeper
Periploca graeca, probably	Periploca
Philadelphus coronarius	Mock Orange, Syringa, Pipe Tree—In 1597 John Gerarde in his "Herball" calls *Philadelphus* a "Syringa" or "White Pipe Tree," he also calls the Lilac "Blue Pipe." The name Pipe Tree comes from the fact that pith can be removed from the stem of *Philadelphus* leaving a hollow receptacle that was made into a pipe.
Pinus sp.	Pine
Platanus occidentalis	Sycamore, Plane-Tree or Large Buttonwood
Platanus orientalis	Oriental Plane Tree
Populus sp.	Poplar
Prunus laurocerasus	Cherry-laurel

128   SHRUBS, TREES, AND VINES—1600–1699 (Continued)

Prunus serotina	Wild Cherry
Pyracantha coccinea, probably	Pyracantha or Coral Tree
Quercus alba	White Oak
Quercus borealis	Red Oak, *Quercus rubra* in literature
Quercus coccinea	Scarlet Oak
Robinia pseudoacacia	Locust
Rosa canina	Dog Rose
Rosa centifolia	Cabbage Rose
Rosa damascena	Damask Rose
Rosa damascena var. *versicolor*	York and Lancaster Rose
Rosa eglanteria	Rose, Sweet Briar, Eglantine
Rosa gallica	French Rose
Rosa gallica var. *versicolor*	Rosamundi Rose
Rosa moschata	Musk Rose
Rosa pomifera	Apple Rose
Rosa sempervirens, probably	Evergreen Rose
Sassafras albidum	Sassafrass
Sorbus domestica or *torminalis*	Service Tree or Sorbus, "liked as a fruit tree"
Staphylea pinnata, probably	Bladder-nut, "beareth sweet whitish flowers"
Syringa vulgaris	Syringa, Pipe Tree, Lilac, Blue Pipe—See *Philadelphus coronarius*.
Thuja occidentalis	Arbor-vitae or Northern White Cedar
Tilia sp., probably *platyphyllos* or *europa*	Linden or Lime
Tsuga canadensis	Canada Hemlock or Pine or Fir Hemlock
Viburnum opulus var. *roseum*	Guelder Rose or Gelder—Other viburnums were also called by this common name, but it seems to have been most associated with this species.

VEGETABLES AND FIELD CROPS—1600–1699

Allium cepa	Onion
Allium porrum	Leeks
Allium sativum	Garlic
Asparagus officinalis	Asparagus
Avena sativa	Oats
Beta vulgaris	Beet
Brassica oleracea var. *botrytis*	Cauliflower, Cole-flower
Brassica oleracea var. *capitata*	Cabbage, Savoy—The variety Savoy is mentioned repeatedly and is still available today.
Brassica rapa	Turnip
Campanula rapunculus	Rampion
Cannabis sativa	Hemp
Cicorium intybus	Wild Endive, Succory
Citrullus vulgaris	Melon
Cucumis melo	Musk Melon
Cucumis sativus	Cucumber
Cucurbita sp.	Squash

Cucurbita pepo	Pumpkin, Pompion
Cynara scolymus	Artichoke
Daucus carota	Carrot
Helianthus tuberosus	Jerusalem Artichoke
Hordeum vulgare	Barley
Humulus lupulus	Hops
Lactuca sativa	Lettuce
Nicotiana tabacum	Tobacco
Pastinaca sativa	Parsnip
Petroselinum crispum	Parsley
Phaseolus vulgaris	Bean
Pisum sativum	Pea
Raphanus sativus	Radish
Secale cereale	Rye
Solanum tuberosum	Potato
Spinacia oleracea	Spinach
Triticum aestivum	Wheat
Zea mays	Corn, "Corne," Maize

FRUITS AND NUTS—1600–1699

Berberis vulgaris	Barberry, Oxycantha or Berberry
Citrus aurantium	Orange
Corylus americana	Hazel or Hazelnut
Corylus maxima	Filberts or Bilbeards
Cydonia oblonga	Quince
Ficus carica	Fig
Fragaria virginiana	Strawberry
Juglans sp.	Walnut
Malus pumila, hybrid derivations from this species	Apple
Mespilus germanica	Medlar
Morus sp.	Mulberry
Prunus amygdalus	Almond
Prunus armeniaca	Apricot or Apricock
Prunus cerasus	Cherry, Sour Cherry
Prunus domestica	Plum, "white, red, blue, being almost as good as the Damson"
Prunus persica	Peach
Prunus persica var. *nectarina*	Nectarine
Punica granatum	Pomegranate
Pyrus communis	Pear or Peare
Ribes grossularia	Gooseberry
Ribes sativum	Currant
Rubus idaeus	Raspberry
Sambucus canadensis	Elderberry or Eldern
Vitis vinifera	Grapes, "white and red, blew, muscadine"

HERBS—AROMATIC, CULINARY AND MEDICINAL—1600–1776

Achillea millefolium	Yarrow
Allium schoenoprasium	Chives, Chibbals, Cives

130   HERBS—AROMATIC, CULINARY AND MEDICINAL—1600–1776   (Continued)

Anchusa sempervirens	Alkanet, Bugloss
Anethum graveolens	Dill
Angelica archangelica	Angelica
Anthemis nobilis	Chamomile
Anthriscus cerefolium	Chervil
Artemisia abrotanum	Southernwood
Artemisia dracunculus	Tarragon
Borago officinalis	Borage
Brassica, probably *juncea*	Mustard
Calendula officinalis	Calendula, Marygold, Pot Marygold
Carum carvi	Caraway
Chrysanthemum balsamita	Costmary, Bibleleaf
Coriandrum sativum	Coriander
Crocus sativus	Saffron
Foeniculum vulgare	Fennel
Glycyrrhiza glabra	Licorice, Liquorice
Hyssopus officinalis	Hyssop, Isop
Isatis tinctoria	Woad, Weld or Dyer's Woad
Lavandula officinalis	Lavender
Lepidium sativum	Cress
Levisticum officinale	Lovage
Linum usitatissimum	Flax
Melissa officinalis	Balm
Mentha sp.	Mints, Garden Mints, "divers sorts"
Mentha spicata	Spearmint
Myrrhis odorata	Sweet Cicely
Nepeta cataria	Catmint, Catnip
Nicotiana tabacum, Nicotiana rustica	Tobacco
Ocimum basilicum	Basil
Ophrys apifera	Bee-flower
Petroselinium crispum var. *latifolium*	Parsley
Pimpinella anisum	Anise
Portulaca oleracea	Purslane
Rheum rhaponticum	Rhubarb
Rosmarinus officinalis	Rosemary
Rubia tinctorum	Madder
Rumex acetosa	Sorrel
Rumex, probably *patientia*	Dock
Ruta graveolens	Rue
Salvia officinalis	Sage
Salvia sclarea	Clary
Sanguisorba officinalis	Burnett
Santolina chamaecyparissus	Santolina, or Lavender Cotton
Satureja, probably both *hortensis* and *montana*	Savory
Sempervivum tectorum, probably	Houseleek
Sisum sisarum	Skirret
Symphytum officinale	Comfrey

Tanacetum vulgare	Tansy	131
Thymus serpyllum	Thyme, Time	

FLOWERS—1700–1776

Adiantum pedatum	Maidenhair Fern
Anaphalis margaritacea	Everlasting Flowers or Pearl Everlasting
Aquilegia canadensis	Columbine
Arctostaphylos uva-ursi	Bear Berry
Argemone grandiflora	Prickly Poppy
Callistephus chinensis	China Aster
Celosia argentea, Celosia argentea var. *cristata, Celosia argentea* var. *plumosa*	Cockscomb
Chelone glabra	Turtlehead
Coreopsis lanceolata	Coreopsis, Tickseed
Delphinium ajacis or *consolida*	Larkspur or Delphinium
Dianthus caryophyllus	Carnations
Dianthus plumarius	Grass Pinks, Cottage Pink
Draba verna	Whitlow Grass
Galanthus nivalis	Snowdrop
Galax aphylla	Galix
Gallium luteum	Yellow Bedstraw
Geranium maculatum	Crane's-bill
Geranium robertianum	Crane's-bill, Herb-Robert or Red Robin
Helianthus annuus	Sunflower
Hibiscus moscheutos	Rose Mallow
Hyacinthus orientalis	Purple Hyacinth
Hypericum linarifolium	Flax-leaved St. John's Wort
Impatiens balsamina	Balsam, "double"
Iris cristata	Dwarf Iris
Iris pallida	Iris, one of the most important sources of tall bearded irises of gardens
Iris pseudacorus	Yellow Iris
Lathyrus maritimus	Beach Pea
Lathyrus odoratus	Annual Sweet Pea
Lunaria annua	Lunaria, Moonwort, Honesty
Lychnis dioica	Catchfly, Morning Campion, Red Campion
Lynchis viscaria	Catchfly, German Catchfly
Lysimachia nummularia	Creeping Jenny, Creeping Charley, Moneywort
Mertensia virginica	Virginia Bluebells
Monarda didyma	Bee Balm
Muscari comosum var. *monstrosum*	Feathered Hyacinth
Narcissus jonquilla	Narcissus or Jonquil
Narcissus poeticus	Poets Narcissus
Oenothera biennis	Evening Primrose
Paeonia suffruticosa	Tree Peony
Papaver orientale	Oriental Poppy
Phlox divaricata	Blue Phlox
Phlox glaberrima	Phlox

FLOWERS—1700–1776 (Continued)

Phlox maculata	Phlox
Phlox paniculata	Summer Phlox or Lychnidea
Poa agrostis	Bent Grass
Primula vulgaris	English Primroses
Rudbeckia hirta	Black-eyed Susan
Saponaria officinalis	Bouncing Bet, Soapwort
Saururus cernuus	Lizard's Tail
Scilla hispanica	Squill, Spanish Bluebell
Scilla sibirica	Siberian Squill
Senecio aureus	Golden Ragwort
Sternbergia lutea	Fall Daffodil—By 1806 the common name of Yellow Amaryllis is also used.
Stokesia laevis	Stokes Aster
Tiarella cordifolia	Foamflower
Trollius asiaticus	Trollius
Typha latifolia	Cat-tail
Valeriana officinalis	Valerian
Verbena officinalis	Vervain
Veronica maritima or longifolia	Veronica
Vinca minor	Periwinkle
Viola canadensis, cucullata, hastata, palmata, pedata, scabriuscula, sororia, striata	Violets

SHRUBS, TREES, AND VINES—1700–1776

Abies balsamea	Balsam
Acacia farnesiana	Egyptian Acacia
Acer negundo	Box Elder
Acer pennsylvanicum	Moosewood, Striped Maple
Acer platanoides	Norway Maple
Acer saccharinum	Silver Maple
Acer saccharum	Sugar Maple
Aesculus hippocastanum	Horse Chestnut, "roasted and eaten to stop the flux"
Aesculus octandra	Sweet Buckeye
Aesculus pavia	Dwarf Horse Chestnut, Red Buckeye
Alnus rugosa	Alder
Amelanchier canadensis	Shadblow, Service Tree or Shad-bush
Amelanchier ovalis	Snowy Mespilus
Amorpha fruticosa	Amorpha, Bastard Indigo, False Indigo
Aralia spinosa	Aralia or Devil's Walking Stick
Aronia arbutifolia	Red Chokeberry
Artemesia abrotanum	Southernwood, Old Man
Asimina triloba	Pawpaw
Baccharis halimifolia	Groundsel Tree
Berberis vulgaris	Barberry
Betula lenta	Black Birch
Betula nigra	River Birch

Bignonia capreolata	Cross-vine	
Broussonetia papyrifera	Common Paper Mulberry	
Buxus sempervirens arborescens	Tree Box	
Buxus sempervirens aurea maculata	Gilded Box	
Buxus sempervirens pendula	Weeping Box	
Buxus sempervirens suffruticosa	Dwarf Box	
Callicarpa americana	Callicarpa, French Mulberry, American Beautyberry	
Calycanthus floridus	Carolina Allspice, Sweetshrub or Sweet-scented Shrub	
Caragana arborescens	Siberian Peashrub	
Carpinus caroliniana	American Hornbeam	
Carya laciniosa	Shell-bark Hickory	
Carya ovata	Scaly-bark Hickory	
Carya pecan	Pecan, Mississippi Nut	
Castanea pumila	Chinquapin	
Catalpa bignonioides	Catalpa, Southern Catalpa	
Ceanothus americanus	New Jersey Tea	
Cedrus libani	Cedar of Lebanon	
Celastrus scandens	American Bittersweet, Climbing Staff Tree, Waxwork, False or Shrubby Bittersweet	
Cephalanthus occidentalis	Button Bush	
Chamaecyparis thyoides	Atlantic White Cedar	
Chimonanthus praecox	Wintersweet	
Chionanthus virginica	Fringe Tree	
Clematis virginiana	Clematis, Virgin's Bower	
Clethra alnifolia	Clethra, Sweet Pepper Bush	
Comptonia peregrina	Sweet Fern	
Cornus alba	White Cornel, White-berried Dogwood, Tartarian Dogwood	
Cornus alba sibirica	Siberian Dogwood	
Cornus florida rubra	Pink Flowering Dogwood	
Coronilla emerus	Emerus	
Crataegus crus-galli	Hawthorn, Cock-spur, Haw	
Crataegus oxycantha	Hawthorn, English Hawthorn	
Crataegus phaenopyrum	Hawthorn, Washington Thorn	
Crataegus punctatus	Large-berried Thorn, Great-fruited Thorn	
Cyrilla racemiflora	Swamp Cyrilla	
Cytisus scoparius	Scotch Broom	
Diospyros virginiana	Persimmon	
Dirca palustris	Leatherwood	
Elaeagnus angustifolia	Russian Olive, Narrow-leaved Oleaster	
Euonymus atropurpureus	Burning Bush	
Exochorda racemosa	Pearl Bush	
Fagus grandifolia	American Beech	
Fagus sylvatica	European Beech	
Fothergilla gardeni	Dwarf Fothergilla	
Franklinia alatamaha	Franklinia—It was grown by John Bartram in his botanical garden but never used extensively in garden plantings.	

134 SHRUBS, TREES, AND VINES—1700–1776 (Continued)

Fraxinus americana	American or White Ash
Fraxinus excelsior	European Ash
Gleditsia triacanthos	Honey Locust
Gymnocladus dioica	Kentucky Coffee Tree, Kentucky Coffeebean
Halesia carolina	Carolina Silver-bell, Snowdrop Tree
Hedera helix	English Ivy
Hydrangea aborescens	Hydrangea
Hypericum calycinum	St. John's Wort
Ilex aquifolium	Evergreen English Holly
Ilex cassine	Dahoon
Ilex decidua	Swamp Holly, Possumhaw
Ilex glabra	Inkberry
Ilex opaca	Evergreen, American Holly
Ilex verticillata	Winterberry, Swamp Red-berry Bush—Winterberry is mentioned before 1700 and is probably either this plant or *I. glabra*.
Ilex vomitoria	Cassine, Cassioberry, Yaupon, Cassena
Itea virginica	Virginian Willow, Sweet Spire
Jasminum officinale	White Flowered Jassmine
Juglans cinerea	Butternut
Juniperus chinensis	Chinese Juniper
Juniperus communis	Juniper
Kalmia latifolia	Mountain Laurel, Ivy Laurel
Koelreuteria paniculata	Golden Rain Tree
Lagerstroemia indica	Crape Myrtle
Laurus nobilis	Sweet Bay, Laurel
Leucothoe axillaris	Leucothoe
Lonicera tartarica	Tartarian Honeysuckle
Lyonia ligustrina	Andromeda
Maclura pomifera	Osage Orange
Magnolia acuminata	Cucumber Tree
Magnolia grandiflora	Southern Magnolia, Carolina Laurel
Magnolia tripetala	Umbrella Magnolia
Malus coronaria	Anchor Tree
Melia azedarach	Chinaberry, Pride of China, Bead Tree
Myrica gale	Bayberry, Sweet Gale
Nerium oleander	Oleander, Rose Bay
Nyssa sylvatica	Sour Gum, Pepperidge, Black Gum, Tupelo or Black Tupelo
Ostrya virginiana	Ironwood, Hop Tree
Oxydendrum arboreum	Sourwood, Sorrel Tree, Andromeda Tree
Persea borbonia	Redbay or Bull Bay
Persea palustris	Swamp Redbay
Pinus nigra	Austrian pines
Pinus strobus	White Pine
Pinus taeda	Loblolly Pine
Pinus virginiana	Virginia Scrub Pine

Populus deltoides	Eastern Poplar	135
Potentilla fruticosa	Potentilla	
Prunus caroliniana	Cherry Laurel	
Prunus cerasifera	Cherry Plum, Myrobalan Plum	
Prunus domestica var. *institia*	Bullace Plum, Damson Plum	
Prunus glandulosa	Flowering Almond	
Prunus maritima	Beach Plum	
Ptelea trifoliata	Trefoil, Hop Tree	
Punica granatum var. *nana*	Bantum Pomegranate	
Pyracantha coccinea	Scarlet or Everlasting Firethorn—Pyracantha referred to before 1700 but without scientific name, probably is this one.	
Quercus falcata	Southern Red Oak	
Quercus marilandica	Blackjack Oak	
Quercus nigra	Water Oak	
Quercus phellos	Willow Oak	
Quercus prinus	Chestnut Oak, Swamp Chestnut Oak, Basket or Cow Oak	
Quercus velutina	Black Oak	
Quercus virginiana	Live Oak	
Rhododendron calendulaceum	Flame Azalea	
Rhododendron indicum	Indica Azalea	
Rhododendron nudiflorum	Wild Honeysuckle, Pinxterbloom Azalea, Upright American Honeysuckle	
Rhododendron viscosum	Swamp White Azalea	
Rhus aromatica	Fragrant Sumac	
Rhus toxicodendron	Poison Oak	
Robinia hispida	Pink Locust, Roseacacia Locust	
Rosa laevigata	Cherokee Rose	
Rosa palustris	Wild Rose, Swamp Rose	
Rosa spinosissima	Scotch Rose	
Ruscus aculeatus	Butchersbroom or Prickly Butcher's Broom	
Salix alba var. *vitellina*	Yellow Willow	
Salix babylonica	Weeping Willow	
Salix caprea	Goat Willow	
Salix repens var. *rosmarinifolia*	Rosemary-leaved Willow	
Sambucus canadensis	American Elder	
Sophora japonica	Japanese Pagoda Tree	
Spartium junceum	Spanish Broom	
Spirea tomentosa	Spirea or Hardhack	
Stewartia malachodendron	Stewartia	
Stewartia ovata	Mountain Stewartia	
Symphoricarpos orbiculatus	Indian Currant or Indiancurrent, Coralberry	
Syringa persica	Lilac, Persian or Persian Jasmine	
Taxodium distichum	Bald or Deciduous Cypress	
Taxus baccata	English Yew	
Taxus canadensis	American Yew	
Tilia americana	American Linden	
Tilia europaea	Linden, or European Lime	

SHRUBS, TREES, AND VINES—1700–1776 (Continued)

Ulmus alata	Winged Elm
Ulmus americana	American Elm
Vaccinium vitis-idaea	Cowberry or Lingon, European Red Huckleberry, Bill-berry
Viburnum acerifolium	Mapleleaf Viburnum
Viburnum cassinoides	Witherod
Viburnum dentatum	Arrowwood
Viburnum lantana	Wayfaring Tree
Viburnum lentago	Nanyberry or Sheepberry
Viburnum prunifolium	Black Haw, Blackhaw Viburnum
Vitex agnus-castus	Chaste Tree
Vitis rotundifolia	Muscadine Grape
Wisteria frutescens	American Wisteria

VEGETABLES AND FIELD CROPS—1700–1776

Apium graveolens var. *dulce*	Celery
Brassica napa	Rape
Brassica oleracea var. *botrytis*	Broccoli
Capsicum frutescens var. *longum*	Cayenne Pepper, Guinea Pepper
Cochlearia officinalis	Scurvy Grass
Dioscorea alata	Yam
Fagopyrum esculentum	Buckwheat
Gossypium herbaceum	Cotton
Hibiscus esculentus	Okra
Indigofera anil	West Indian Indigo
Indigofera tinctoria	Indigo
Lagenaria	Squash, Calabash-Bottle Gourd
Lens esculenta	Lentil
Lepidium sativum	Pepper Grass, Garden Cress
Rumex acetosa	Sorrel
Vicia sp.	Vetch
Vigna sinensis	Black-eyed Pea

FRUITS AND NUTS—1700–1776

Castanea dentata	Chestnut
Castanea sativa	French Chestnut
Diospyrus virginiana	Persimmon
Juglans nigra	Black Walnut
Juglans regia	English Walnut
Malus angustifolia	Crab Apple
Morus alba	White Mulberry
Morus nigra	English Mulberry, Blackberry Tree
Morus rubra	Red or American Mulberry
Olea europaea	Olive
Ribis nigrum	European Black Currant

Rubus sp.	Blackberry, collected from the wild but not cultivated 137
Vaccinium macrocarpum	Cranberry, gathered but not cultivated

ANNUALS AND PERENNIALS—1776–1850

Achillea ptarmica, fl. pl.	Double Sneezewort
Aconitum lycoctonum	Great Yellow Monk's Hood, Wolfsbane
Aconitum napellus var. *album*	White Monk's Hood
Aconitum uncinatum	American Monk's Hood, Wolfsbane
Actea spicata	Herb Christopher, White Snakeroot, Black Baneberry
Adlumia fungosa	Spongy-flowered Fumitory, Climbing Fumitory, Mountain Fringe, Allegheny-vine
Adonis aestivalis	Tall Adonis, Summer Adonis
Adonis autumnalis	Flos Adonis, Bird's Eye, Pheasant's Eye
Adonis vernalis	Perennial Adonis, Pheasants-eye, Spring Adonis
Adoxa moshatellina	Tuberous Moschatel, Musk-root
Agnostemma githago	Corn Rose Campion, Corn Cockle
Allionia sp.	Glacous Allionia
Allium moly	Yellow Garlick, Molly
Allium oleraceum	Purple-striped Garlick
Allium ramosum or *tuberosum*	Sweet-scented Garlick
Allium roseum	Rose Garlick
Alyssum halimifolium	Sweet Alyssum
Amaranthus hybridus, var. *hypochondriacus*	Blue Amethyst, Prince's Feather
Amethystea caerulea	Blue Amethyst
Anagallis arvensis	Red Pimpernel, Poor Man's Weatherglass
Anarrhinum bellidifolium	Daisy-leaved Toad-flax
Anemone hortensis	Garden Anemone
Anemonella thalictroides	Rue-anemone
Apocynum androsaemifolium	Tutsan-leaved Dog's-bane, Spreading Dogbane
Aquilegia alpina	Alpine Columbine
Aquilegia vulgaris	European Columbine
Arctotis sp.	Chamomile Arctotis
Arethusa bulbosa	Bulbous Arethusa
Argemone mexicana	Prickley Argemone
Arisaema triphyllum	Indian Turnep, Three-leaved Arum, Jack-in-the-pulpit
Armeria maritima var. *elongata*	Sea Pink, Statice Armeria
Armeria plantaginea	Plantain-leaved Thrift
Aruncus sylvester	Goat's-beard Spiraea
Asclepias incarnata	Flesh-colored Swallow-wort, Swamp Milkweed
Asclepias purpurascens	Purple Virginian Swallow-wort
Asclepias rubra	Red Swallow-wort
Asclepias syriaca	Syrian Swallow-wort
Asclepias tuberosa, probably	Pleuresy-root, Butterfly-weed
Asclepias verticillata	Verticillate Swallow-wort, Horsetail Milkweed
Asphodelus ramosus	Branched Asphodel
Aster alpinus	Alpine Starwort, "above 50 other sp."
Aster grandiflorus	Catesby's Starwort

Aster novae-angliae	New England Starwort, New England Aster
Aster undulatus	Waved Starwort
Astragalus galegiformis	Goat's-rue-leaved Astragalus
Aureolaria flava	Yellow-flowered Gerardia
Aureolaria pedicularia	Louse-wort-leaved Gerardia
Baptisia alba	White Podalyria, White False or Wild Indigo
Baptisia australis	Blue or Sophora Podalyria, False or Wild Indigo
Baptisia tinctoria	Yellow Podalyria, Bastard Indigo
Browallia americana	Upright Browallia, blue and white
Bupleurum rotundifolia	Round-leaved Hare's ear, Thorough-wax
Bupthalmum grandiflorum	Great-flowered Ox-eye
Calceolaria pinnata	Pinnated Slipper-wort
Calonyction aculeatum	Prickly Ipomoea or Common Moonflower
Calopogon fulchellus	Tuberous-rooted Limodorum, Grass-pink Orchid
Caltha palustris var. *monstrosa-pleno*	Double Marsh Marigold
Campanula carpatica	Heart-leaved Bell-flower, Tussock Bell-flower
Campanula glomerata	Clustered Bell-flower
Campanula persicifolia var. *grandiflora*	Great-flowered Bell-flower
Campanula pyramidalis	Pyramidal Bell-flower, Chimney Bell-flower
Campanula rapunculoides	Nettle-leaved Bell-flower, Rover Bell-flower
Campanula trachelium	Great Bell-flower
Cardamine pratensis	Double Ladies-smock or Cuckoo-flower
Cardiospermum halicacabum	Smooth-leaved Heart-seed, Balloon-vine
Carpanthea pomeridiana	Great Yellow-flowered Fig Marigold
Carthamus tinctorius	Bastard Saffron, Safflower, False Saffron
Cassia fasciculata	Dwarf Cassia, Partridge Pea
Cassia marilandica	Maryland Cassia, Wild Senna
Catananche caerulea	Blue Catananche
Celsia orientalis	Oriental Celsia
Centaurea alpina	Alpine Centaury
Centaurea glastifolia	Woad-leaved Centaury
Centaurea montana	Mountain Blue-bottle, Mountain Bluet
Centaurea moschata	Sweet Purple Sultan, Sweet Sultan
Centaurea moschata var. *alba*	White Sweet Sultan
Centaurium sp.	American Centaury
Centranthus ruber	Red Garden Valerian, Jupiter's Beard
Cerinthe major	Great Purple Honey-wort
Chelone obliqua	Red Chelone
Chenepodium botrys	Sweet-scented Goosefoot, Feather Geranium, Jerusalem Oak
Chenopodium capitatum	Berry-headed Blite
Chrysanthemum carinatum	Three-coloured Chrysanthemum
Chrysanthemum coronarium	Garden Chrysanthemum, Garland Chrysanthemum, Crown Daisy
Chrysanthemum indicum	Indian Chrysanthemum
Chrysoplenium alternafolium	Alternate-leaved Golden Saxifrage
Cimicifuga racemosa	Black Snake Root

Claytonia virginica	Virginian Claytonia	139
Clematis integrifolia	Entire-leaved Virgin's Bower	
Clematis ochroleuca	Yellow-flowered Virgin's Bower	
Clematis recta	Upright Virgin's Bower	
Cleome sp.	Five-leaved Cleome	
Cleome sp.	Violet-coloured Cleome	
Coix lacryma-jobi	Job's Tears	
Convolvulus tricolor	Minor Convolvulus, Dwarf Morning Glory	
Coreopsis auriculata	Ear-leaved Coreopsis	
Coreopsis verticillata	Whorl-leaved Coreopsis, Thread-leaf Coreopsis	
Coronilla varia	Purple Coronilla, Crown Vetch	
Corydalis capnoides, probably	White-flowered Fumitory	
Corydalis cava	Hollow Rooted Fumitory	
Corydalis cava, var. *bulbosa*	Bulbous Fumitory	
Corydalis lutea, probably	Yellow Fumitary	
Corydalis sempervirens	Glaucous Fumitory, Roman Wormwood	
Crepis rubra	Red Hawkweed, Hawks Beard	
Crocus susianus	Crocus, Cloth of Gold	
Cryophytum nodiflorum	Egyptian Fig Marigold	
Cryptostemma calendulaceum	Marigold-flowered Arctotis	
Cucumis melo var. *dudaim*	Dudaim Cucumber, "highly perfumed"	
Cucumis melo var. *flexuosus*	Snake or Melon Cucumber, "grown as a curiosity"	
Cucurbita pepo var. *ovifera*	Egg Gourd, "many forms and colors of small hard-shelled ornamental durable fruits"	
Cypripedium acaule	Two-leaved Purple Lady's Slipper, Pink Lady's Slipper	
Cypripedium calceolus	English Lady's Slipper, Yellow Lady-slipper of Eurasia	
Datura metel	Double Purple Stramonium	
Delphinium elatum	Bee Larkspur	
Delphinium elatum var. *intermedium*	Palmated Bee Larkspur	
Delphinium exaltatum	American Larkspur	
Dianthus carthusianorum	Carthusian Pink, Clusterhead Pink	
Dianthus chinensis	China Pink, Rainbow Pink	
Dianthus deltoides	Maiden or Common Pink	
Dianthus superbus	Superb Pink	
Dicentra cucullaria	Naked-stalked Fumitory or Dutchman's Breeches	
Dictamnus albus var. *rubra*	Red-flowered Fraxinella, Dittany, Gasplant, Burning Bush	
Digitalis ferruginea	Iron-coloured Fox-glove, Rusty Fox-glove	
Digitalis lutea	Small Yellow Fox-glove, Straw Foxglove	
Digitalis purpurea var. *alba*	White-flowered Fox-glove	
Dimorphotheca annua	Small Cape Marigold	
Dimorphotheca hybrida	Large Cape Marigold	
Dodecatheon meadia	American Cowslip, Shooting Star	
Dolichus lablab	Black-seeded Dolichus, Hyacinth Bean, Bonavist Lablab	
Dracocephalum austriacum	Austrian Dragon's Head	
Dracocephalum grandiflorum	Great-flowered Dragon's Head	

Dracocephalum moldavica	Moldavian Balm
Dracocephalum nutans	Nodding Dragon's Head
Dracocephalum thymiflorum	Thyme-leaved Dragon's Head
Ecballium elaterium	Squirting Cucumber
Echinacea angustifolia	Narrow-leaved Rudbeckia
Echinacea purpurea	Purple Rudbeckia, Purple Coneflower
Echinops ritro	Small Globe Thistle
Echinops sphaerocephalus	Great Globe Thistle
Emilia sagittata	Scarlet-flowered Cacalia, Tassel Flower, Flora's Paintbrush
Epilobium angustifolium	Narrow-leaved Willow-herb, Fireweed, Giant Willow-herb
Eryngium alpinum	Alpine Eryngium
Erythronium americanum	American Erythronium
Eupatorium altissimum	Tall Eupatorium
Eupatorium coelestinum	Blue-flowered Eupatorium, Mist Flower, "there are many others"
Euphorbia lathyrus	Caper Spurge, Mole Plant, "there are many others"
Euphorbia marginata	Snow-on-the-mountain
*Filipendula hexapetala**	Filipendula or Dropwort
Filipendula ulmaria	Meadow Sweet, Queen-of-the-meadow
Fritillaria camschatcensis	Kamptschatka Lily
Fritillaria pyrenaica	Black Fritillary
Galega officinalis	Goat's-rue or Officinal Galega
Gaura sp.	Biennial Gaura
Gentiana acaulis	Dwarf Gentian, Gentianella, Stemless Gentian
Gentiana crinita	Fringed-flowered Gentian, Fringed Gentian
Gentiana lutea	Yellow Gentian
Gentiana purpurea	Purple Gentian
Gentiana saponaria	Soap-wort-leaved Gentian
Gentiana villosa	Hoary Gentian
Geranium aconitifolium	Aconite-leaved Geranium
Geranium macrorrhizum	Large-rooted Crane's-bill
Geranium striatum	Streaked Geranium
Gladiolus communis	European Corn-flag*
Gladiolus segetum	Round-seeded Corn-flag, Cornflag
Glaucium flavum	Yellow Horned Poppy, Sea Poppy
Globularia cordifolia	Cordate-leaved Globularia
Globularia vulgaris	European Globularia or Blue Daisy
Hedysarum coronarium	French Honeysuckle
Helenium autumnale	Smooth Helenium, Sneezeweed
Helianthus annuus var. *nanus*	Dwarf Annual Sunflower
Helianthus atrorubens	Dark Red Sunflower, Dark-eye Sunflower
Helianthus decapetalus	Many-flowered Perennial Sunflower, Thin-leaf Sunflower
Helianthus giganteus	Gigantic Sunflower
Helleborus foetidus	Stinking Bear's-foot

Helleborus, probably *orientalis*	Livid or Purple Hellebore	141
Helleborus viridis	Green Hellebore	
Helonias bullata	Spear-leaved Helonias, Swamp Pink	
Hepatica americana or *nobilis*	Common Hepatica, Liverleaf	
Hermodactylus tuberosus	Snakes-head Iris	
Hesperis tristis	Night Smiling Rocket	
Heuchera americana	American Heuchera or Sanicle, Alum Root	
Hibiscus militaris	Halbert-leaved Hibiscus, Soldier Rose Mallow	
Hibiscus speciosus	Special Smooth Hibiscus	
Hibiscus trionum	Bladder Hibiscus, Ketmia, Flower-of-an-hour	
Hippocrepis multisiliquosa	Many-podded or Horseshoe Vetch	
Houstonia caerulea	Blue Flowered Houstonia, Bluets	
Houstonia purpurea	Purple-flowered Houstonia	
Hyacinthus amethystinus	Amethyst-coloured Hyacinth	
Hyacinthus romanus	Roman Grape Hyacinth	
Hydrastis canadensis	Canadian Yellow-root, Goldenseal, Orange Root	
*Hypericum calycinum**	Large-flowered St. John's-wort	
Hypericum hirsutum	Hairy St. John's-wort	
Hypoxis hirsuta	Upright Hypoxis	
Iberis amara	White Candy-tuft, Rocket Candy-tuft	
Iberis odorata	Sweet-scented Candy-tuft	
Iberis umbellata	Purple Candy-tuft, Globe Candy-tuft—First species introduced. Brought from Candia, thus the name.	
Impatiens noli-tangere	Touch Me Not	
Ipomoea purpurea	Common Morning Glory	
Iris fulva	Copper Iris, Red Iris	
Iris pumila	Iris, Dwarf Flag	
Iris sibirica	Siberian Iris	
Iris sisyrinchium	Crocus-rooted Iris	
Iris versicolor	Various-colored Iris	
Iris virginica	Virginian Iris	
Iris xiphium	Iris, Spanish Flag, Bulbous Iris	
Ixia chinensis	Chinese Ixia	
Jeffersonia diphylla	Binate-leaved Jeffersonia, Twin-leaf	
Kickxia elatine	Fluellin, Toad-flax	
Kochia scoparia	Belvedere, Summer Cypress	
Lathyrus sativus	Blue Chickling Vetch, Grass Pea	
Lathyrus tingitanus	Tangier Pea	
Lavatera thuringiaca	Great-flowered Lavatera	
Lavatera trimestris	European Lavatera	
Leucojum aestivum	Summer Snowdrop	
Leucojum autumnale	Autumnal Snowdrop	
Liatris elegans, probably	Hairy-cupped Liatris—Liatris is also known as Blazing Star, Gayfeather, or Button Snakeroot.	
Liatris pilosa	Hairy-leaved Liatris	
Liatris spicata	Long-spiked Liatris	
Lilium candidum	Common White Lily, Madonna Lily	
Lilium catesbaei	Catesby's Lily, Southern Red Lily	
Lilium croceum	Bulb-bearing or Orange Lily	

Authentic Plants for Period Landscape Settings

Lilium philadelphicum	Philadelphia Lily, Orangecup Lily, Wood Lily
Lilium pomponium	Pomponean Lily
Lilium speciosum	Speciosum Lily
Lilium superbum	Superb Lily, American Turks Cap Lily
Linaria purpurea	Purple Toad-flax
Linum perenne	Perennial Flax
Lobelia siphilitica	Blue Cardinal's Flower
Lobularia maritima, probably	Sweet Alyssum
Lopezia coronata	Mexican Lopezia
Lotus tetragonolobus	Winged Pea
Lupinus albus	White Annual Lupin
Lupinus angustifolius	Narrow-leaved Blue Lupin
Lupinus hirsutus	Great Blue Lupin
Lupinus luteus	Yellow Lupin
Lupinus perennis	Perennial Lupin, Sun Dial Lupin
Lupinus pilosus	Rose Lupin
Lupinus varius	Small Blue Lupin
Lychnis coeli-rosa	Smooth-leaved Rose Campion, Rose-of-heaven
Lychnis flos-cuculi	Meadow Lychnis, Cuckoo Flower or Ragged Robin
Lychnis flos-jovis	Umbelled Campion, Flower of Jove
Lysimachia quadrifolia	Four-leaved Loose-strife
Lythrum salicaria	Purple European Willow-herb, Purple Loose-strife
Lythrum virgatum	Fine-leaved Willow-herb
Malcomia maritima	Annual Stock or Mediterranean Stock
Malva crispa	Curled Mallow
Medicago intertexta	Medic, Hedghog
Medicago scutellata	Medic, Snail, Snails
Melanthium latifolium	Spear-leaved Melanthium
Melanthium virginicum	Virginian Melanthium, Bunch Flower
Menyanthes trifoliata	English Buck-bean, also Bog Bean
Mimulus alatus	Wing-stalked Monkey-flower
Mimulus ringens	Oblong-leaved Monkey-flower
Mirabilis dichotomo	Forked Marvel of Peru, Marvel of Peru, Four O'Clock
Mirabilis longiflora	Sweet-scented Marvel of Peru
Mirabilis viscosa	Clammy Marvel of Peru
Molucella laevis	Smooth Molucca Balm, Shell Flower
Molucella spinosa	Prickly Molucca Balm
Momordica balsamina	Male Balsam Apple
Momordica charantia	Hairy Balsam Apple, Balsam Pear
Monarda punctata	Yellow-flowered Monarda, Horse Mint
Muscari racemosum	Clustered Grape Hyacinth
Myosotis arvensis	Forget me Not
Narcissus biflorus	Two-flowered Narcissus, Primrose Peerless Narcissus
Narcissus bulbocodium	Hoop-petticoat Narcissus, Petticoat Daffodil
Narcissus moschatus	Musk-scented Narcissus
Narcissus odorus	Sweet-scented Narcissus, Campernelle Jonquil

Narcissus pseudo-narcissus	Common Daffodil, Trumpet Narcissus
N. *Minor*, form bicolor	Small Narcissus
N. *psuedo narcissus*, form bicolor	Two-coloured Narcissus
N. *tazetta*, form bicolor	Two-coloured Narcissus
Narcissus serotinus	Late-flowering Narcissus
Narcissus tazetta	Polyanthus Narcissus
Narcissus tazetta var. *orientalis*	Oriental Narcissus, Chinese Sacred Lily
Narcissus triandrus	Rush-leaved Narcissus, Angels Tears
Nelumbium pentapetalum	Yellow Indian Water Lily, American Lotus, Water Chinkapin
Nigella hispanica	Fenel-flower, Devil in a Bush
Nolana prostrata	Trailing Nolana
Nuphae advenum	Three-coloured Water Lily
Nuphae luteum	Yellow Water Lily
Nymphaea alba	European White Water Lily
Nymphaea odorata	American Sweet-scented White Water Lily
Oenothera fruticosa	Shrubby Primrose-tree
Oenothera perennis	Dwarf Primrose-tree
Oenothera tetraptera	Changeable Primrose-tree
Ophrys apifera	Bee Ophrys
Orchis spectabilis	Shewy Orchis, Showy Orchis
Ornithogalum pyramidale	Pyramidal Star of Bethlehem
Ornithogalum thyrsoides	Yellow Star of Bethlehem
Ornthogalum umbellatum	Umbelled Star of Bethlehem
Oxalis violacea	Purple Oxalis, Wood Sorrel
Oxybaphus sp.	Viscid Umbrella-wort
Paeonia albiflora	White-flowered Peony
Paeonia anomala or a var. of *Paeonia tenuifolia*	Jagged-leaved Peony
Paeonia tenuifolia	Slender-leaved Peony
Pancratium maritimum	Sea Pancratium
Papaver dubium	Smooth Poppy
Papaver rhoeas	Corn Poppy
Papaver somniferum	Common White Poppy, also double-flowered in all sorts
Paradisea liliastrum	St. Bruno's Lily
Passiflora lutea	Yellow Passion-flower
Penstemon hirsutus	Hairy Penstemon
Penstemon laevigatus	Smooth Penstemon
Phaseolus coccineus	Scarlet-flowering Kidney Bean
Phlox carolina	Carolina Phlox, Lychnadea, Thick-leaf Phlox
Phlox drummondii	Annual or Drummond Phlox
Phlox nivalis	Fine-leaved Phlox, Trailing Phlox
Phlox ovata	Oval-leaved Phlox
Phlox pilosa	Hairy Phlox
Phlox stolonifera	Creeping or Daisy-leaved Phlox
Phlox subulata	Awl-shaped Phlox, Ground or Moss Pink
Physostegia virginiana	Virginian Dragon's Head, False Dragon-head
Podophyllum peltatum	May Apple
Polemonium caeruleum	Blue European Valerian, Jacob's Ladder, Greek Valerian, Charity

Authentic Plants for Period Landscape Settings

144 ANNUALS AND PERENNIALS—1776–1850 (Continued)

Polemonium caeruleum var. *album*	White Valerian
Polemonium reptans	Creeping Greek Valerian
Polygala lutea	Yellow Annual Milkwort
Polygala senega	Officinal Milkwort, Seneca Snakeroot, Rattle-snake Root
Polyganatum multiflorum	Many-flowered Solomon's-seal
Polygonum orientale	Tall Persicaria, Princes-Feather
Polygonum persicaria	Persicaria, Ladys-Thumb
Pontederia cordata	Heart-leaved Pontederia, Pickerel-weed
Potentilla grandiflora	Great-flowered Potentilla
Primula elatior	Oxslip or Polyanthus
Primula farinosa	Bird's-eye Cowslip
Primula glutinosa	Clammy Primrose
Primula longiflora	Long-leaved Primrose
Primula marginata	Silver-edged Primrose
Primula polyantha, forma *Hose-in-Hose*	Hose-in-Hose Primrose
Primula veris	Cowslip
Proboscidea sp.	Unicorn Plant or Cuckold's Horns
Prunella grandiflora	Great-flowered Self-heal
Pyrola rotundifolia	Round-leaved Winter-green
Quamoclit coccinea	Scarlet Ipomoea, Star Ipomoea
Quamoclit coccinea var. *hederifolia*	Ivy-leaved Ipomoea
Quamoclit pennata	Cypress Vine, Winged-leaved Ipomoea
Ranunculus aconitifolius	Fair Maids of France
Ranunculus acris, fl. pl.	Double Upright Crowfoot
Ranunculus bulbosus, fl. pl.	Double Bulbous Crowsfoot
Ranunculus ficaria	Pilewort (double and single)
Ranunculus gramineus	Grass-leaved Crowfoot
Reseda odorata	Mignonette
Rhexia mariana	Maryland Rhexia
Rhexia virginica	Hairy-leaved Rhexia
Ricinus communis	Castor-oil Plant, Palma Christi
Rudbeckia fulgida	Bright Rudbeckia
Rudbeckia laciniata	Jagged-leaved Rudbeckia
Rumex patientia	Dock, Patience
Salvia hispanica	Spanish Sage
Salvia lyrata	Lyre-leaved Sage
Saponaria ocymoides	Basil-leaved Soapwort
Sarracenia flava	Yellow Side-saddle Flower, Pitcher Plant
Sarracenia minor	Small Side-saddle Flower
Sarracenia purpurea	Purple Side-saddle Flower
Sarracenia rubra	Red Side-saddle Flower
Saxifraga cotyledon	Pyramidal Saxifrage
Saxifraga granulata	White Granulous-rooted Saxifrage, Meadow Saxifrage
Saxifraga hypnoides	Mossy Saxifrage, Lady's Cushion
Saxifraga sarmentosa	Strawberry Saxifrage, Strawberry Geranium

Saxifraga umbrosa	London Pride
Saxifraga virginiensis	Virginian Saxifrage
Scilla autumnalis	Squill
Scilla bifolia	Two-leaved Squill
Scilla italica	Italian Squill
Scilla peruviana	Squill
Scorpiurus muricata	Two-flowered Caterpillar
Scorpiurus sulcata	Furrowed Caterpillar
Scorpiurus vermiculata	One-flowered Caterpillar
Scutellaria integrifolia	Entire-leaved Scul-cap, Skullcap
Sedum aizoon	Yellow Stonecrop, Live-for-ever, also a common name for Sedums in general
Sedum album	White Stonecrop
Sedum anacampseros	Evergreen Orpine
Sempervivum arachnoideum	Cobweb Houseleek
Sempervivum montanum	Mountain Houseleek
Sempervivum montanum, form *globiferum*	Globular Houseleek
Senecio elegans	Elegant Groundsel, Purple Jacoboea, Purple Ragwort
Sesamum orientale	Oriental Sesamum, Oily-grain, Sesame
Silene alpestris	Austrian Catchfly, Alpine Catchfly
Silene armeria	Lobel's Catchfly, Sweet William Catchfly
Siline caroliniana	Pennsylvanian Catchfly, Wild Pink
Silene pendula	Pendulous Catchfly
Silene virginica	Virginian Catchfly, Fire Pink
Silphium laciniatum	Jagged-leaved Silphium, Compass Plant—Silphiums are also known as Rosinweed.
Silphium perfoliatum	Square-stalked Silphium, Cup Plant, Indian Cup
Silphium terebinthinum	Broad-leaved Silphium, Prairie Dock
Silphium trifoliatum	Three-leaved Silphium
Sisyrinchium bermudiana	Bermudian Sisyrinchium—The plants of this genus are also known as Blue-eyed-grass.
Sisyrinchium graminoides	Grass-leaved Sisyrinchium
Sisyrinchium mucronatum	Pointed Sisyrinchium
Smilacina racemosa, probably	Cluster-flowered Solomon's-seal
Soldanella alpina	Alpine Soldanella
Solidago altissima	Tall Golden-rod
Solidago flexicaulis	Figwort-leaved Golden-rod
Solidago graminifolia	Lance-leaved Golden-rod
Solidago latifolia	Broad-leaved Golden-rod
Solidago odora	Sweet-scented Golden-rod
Specularia speculum-veneris	Venus Looking Glass
Spigelia marilandica	Carolina Pink-root
Stachys grandiflora	Great-flowered Betony—Plants of this genus are also known as Woundworts.
Stachys lanata	Wooly Stachys, Lambs Ears
Teucrium flavum	Tree Germander
Thalictrum dioicum	Dioecious Meadow-rue
Thalictrum polygamum	Meadow-rue
Tolpis barbata	Yellow Hawkweed, Golden Yellow Hawkweed

ANNUALS AND PERENNIALS—1776–1850 (Continued)

Tradescantia virginiana	Virginian Spider-wort, Common Spiderwort
Trifolium incarnatum	Crimson-spiked Clover
Trillium cernum	Nodding-flowered Trillium
Trillium erectum	Erect-flowered Trillium
Trillium pusillum	Dwarf Trillium
Trillium sessile	Sessile-flowered Trillium
Trillium undulatum	Red-fruited Trillium
Triosteum perfoliatum	Fever Root, Horse Gentian, Feverwort
Tulipa sylvestris	Italian Yellow Tulip
Urtica pilulifera	Roman Nettle
Vallisneria americana	American Vallisneria
Vallisneria spiralis	European Vallisneria, Eel Grass, Tape Grass
Veratrum viride	Green-flowered Veratrum
Verbascum blattaria	Moth Mullein
Verbascum phoeniceum	Purple Mullein
Verbesina encelioides	Annual Xeminesia
Veronicastrum virginicum	Virginian Speedwell, Culver's Root
Vicia oroboides	Upright Bitter Vetch
Vigna sesquipedalis	Long-podded Dolichos, Asparagus Bean, Yard Long Bean
Viola lanceolata	Lance-leaved Violet
Viola odorata, fl. pl.	Double Sweet-scented Violet, Sweet Garden or Florist's Violet
Viola primulifolia	Primrose-leaved Violet
Viola pubescens	Downey Violet
Viola rotundifolia	Yellow Round-leaved Violet
Xeranthemum annuum	Eternal Flower, Common Immortelle
Zephyranthes atamasco	Atamasco Lily
Zinnia elegans	Violet-coloured Zinnia, Youth-and-old-age
Zinnia multiflora	Red Zinnia
Zinnia panciflora	Yellow Zinnia

SHRUBS, TREES, AND VINES—1776–1850

Abies alba	Silver Fir
Acer circinatum	Vine Maple
Acer macrophyllum	Big-leaf Maple, Oregon Maple
Acer palmatum	Japanese Maple
Acer platinoides*	Norway Maple
Acer pseudo-platanus	European Sycamore, Sycamore Maple
Acer saccharinum*	Silver Maple
Acer spicatum	Mountain Maple
Aesculus flava	Yellow-flowering Horse Chestnut
Aesculus hippocastanum*	Horse Chestnut
Ailanthus altissima	Tree-of-heaven
Akebia quinata	Five-leaf Akebia, not in the trade until after 1845
Albizzia julibrissin	Silk Tree, Mimosa

Amygdalus persica, fl. pl.	Double-flowering Peach
Aralia elata	Japanese Angelica-tree, introduced in 1830
Araucaria araucana	Monkey-puzzle Tree, introduced in 1795
Aristolochia durior	Dutchman's Pipe
Aucuba japonica variegata	Gold-dust-tree
Berberis canadensis	Canadian Berberry, Allegheny Barberry
Betula lutea	Yellow Birch, Tall Birch
Betula nana	European Dwarf Birch
Betula papyrifera	Canoe or Paper Birch
Betula pendula	Common European or European White Birch
Betula pendula, probably var. *tristis* or *gracilus*	Drooping Birch
Betula populifolia	Poplar-leaved or Gray Birch
Betula pumila	American Hairy Dwarf Birch
Buxus sempervirens angustifolia	Narrow-leaved Box
Calycanthus fertilis var. *ferax*	Pennsylvania Sweet Shrub
Calycanthus floridus*	Carolina Allspice, Sweetshrub, Sweet-scented Shrub
Camellia japonica	Common Camellia, the fashionable specialty of the wealthy in the early 1900s, introduced in 1797.
Carpinus betulus	Common European Hornbeam
Carya glabra	Pignut
Castanea pumila*	Chinquapin
Cedrus atlantica	Atlas Cedar
Cedrus libani*	Cedar of Lebanon
Celtis occidentalis*	American Nettle-tree
Celtis australis	European Nettle-tree
Cercis siliquastrum	European Red-bud
Chaenomeles lagenaria	Flowering Quince
Chamaedaphne calyculata	Globe-flowered Andromeda, Leather Leaf
Cladrastis lutea	Yellow Wood
Clematis alpina	Alpine Clematis
Clematis cirrhosa	Evergreen Virgin's Bower
Clematis crispa	Curled Virgin's Bower
Clematis florida	Cream Clematis
Clematis orientalis	Oriental Virgin's Bower
Clematis viorna	Leathery-flowered Virgin's Bower
Clematis vitalba	English Virgin's Bower, Traveler's Joy, Old Man's Beard
Clethra alnifolia*	Sweet Pepperbush or Summer Sweet
Clethra alnifolia var. *paniculata*	Sweet Pepperbush
Coffea arabica	Coffee
Colutea arborescens	Bladder Sena
Colutea orientalis	Oriental Sena
Coriaria myrtifolia	Myrtle-leaved Sumach
Cornus alba*	Tartarian Dogwood
Cornus alternifolia	Alternate-leaved Dogwood
Cornus foemina	Upright Dogwood
Cornus mas	Cornelian Cherry
Cornus racemosa	Panicled Dogwood
Cornus rugosa	Pennsylvania Dogwood

148   SHRUBS, TREES, AND VINES—1776–1850 (Continued)

Cornus sanguinea	Red-twigged Dogwood, Bloodtwig Dogwood
Cotoneaster microphylla	Small-leaved Cotoneaster, introduced in 1824
Crataegus azarolus	Parsley-leaved Azarole
Crataegus viridis	Green-leaved Virginian Hawthorn
Cynara cardunculus	Spanish Cardoon
Cyrilla racemiflora	Swamp Cyrilla
Cytissus sessilifolius	Sessile-leaved Cytissus
Daphne alpina	Alpine Daphne
Daphne cneorum	Trailing Daphne
Daphne laureola	Evergreen Spurge Laurel
Diospyros lotus	European Date Plum
*Elaeagnus angustifolia**	Narrow-leaved Oleaster, Russian Olive
Elaeagnus angustifolia var. *spinosa*	Thorny Oleaster
Elaeagnus pungens	Thorny Elaeagnus, introduced in 1830
Elaeagnus umbellata	Autumn Elaeagnus, introduced in 1830
Erica carnea	Spring Heath
Euonymus americanus	Evergreen Spindle-tree, Burning Bush
Euonymus europaeus	European Spindletree
Euonymus japonicus	Evergreen Euonymus, introduced in 1804
Euonymus latifolius	Broad-leaved Spindletree
Euonymus verrucosus	Warted Spindletree
Euphorbia pulcherrima	Poinsettia, brought from Mexico to Charleston by Joel Poinsett in 1833
Fatsia japonica	Fatsia, introduced in 1838
Forsythia suspensa sieboldii	Siebold Weeping Forsythia, introduced in 1833
*Fothergilla gardeni**	Dwarf Fothergilla
*Franklinia alatamaha**	Franklinia
Fraxinus caroliniana	Red Ash, Water Ash
Fraxinus, probably *excelsior* var. *pendula*	Drooping Ash
Fraxinus nigra	Black American Ash
Fraxinus ornus	True Manna, Flowering Manna, Flowering Ash
Fraxinus rotundifolia	Round-leaved Manna
Gaultheria procumbens	Mountain Tea, Teaberry, Wintergreen, Checker-berry, Tea-berry
Ginko biloba	Maidenhair Tree
Gleditsia aquatica	One-seeded Locust, Water or Swamp Locust
Gleditsia japonica	Long-spined Locust
Gleditsia sinensis	Chinese Honey-Locust
Gleditsia triacanthos var. *inermis*	Thornless Locust
*Halesia carolina**	Carolina Silver-bell, Snowdrop Tree
Halesia diptera	Two-winged Snowdrop Tree
Hibiscus syriacus	Rose-of-Sharon
Hippophae rhaminoides	Sea Buckthorn
*Hydrangea arborescens**	Hydrangea
Hydrangea macrophylla	House Hydrangea, introduced between 1780 and 1817
Hydrangea radiata	Downy Hydrangea
Hypericum kalmianum	Kalmia-leaved St. John's-wort

Ilex aquifolium var. *ferox*	Hedge-hog Holly, "numerous other varieties, striped, blotched, etc."
Ilex aquifolium var. *heterophylla*	Various-leaved Holly
Ilex aquifolium var. *recurva*	Slender-leaved Holly
Ilex cassine *	Dahoon
Ilex laevigata	Smooth Winterberry
Itea cyrilla	Entire Leaved Itea
Jasminum fruticans	Common Yellow Jasmine
Juglans microcarpa	Texas Black Walnut, probably not cultivated until the end of this period
Juniperus communis var. *suecta*	Swedish Juniper
Kalmia angustifolia	Narrow-leaved Kalmia, Laurel, Lambkill, Sheep Laurel
Kalmia polifolia	Glaucus-leaved Kalmia, Bog Kalmia
Kerria japonica fl. pl.	Crocus Rose, Globe-flower
Koelreuteria paniculata *	Golden Rain Tree
Ledum groenlandicum	Broad-leaved Ledum, Labrador Tea
Ledum palustre	Marsh Ledum, Crystal Tea, Wild Rosemary
Leucothoe axillaris *	Leucothoe
Leucothoe racemosa	Branching Andromeda, Sweetbells
Ligustrum japonicum	Japanese Privet, probably not much used before the end of this period
Ligustrum lucidum	Glossy Privet, introduced between 1780 and 1817
Lonicera caprifolium	Italian Honeysuckle
Lonicera flava	Yellow Honeysuckle
Lonicera japonica	Japanese Honeysuckle, introduced in 1806
Lonicera ledebouri	Ledebour Honeysuckle, introduced in 1838
Lyonia mariana	Maryland Andromeda, Stagger Bush
Magnolia acuminata *	Cucumber Tree
Magnolia denudata	Yulan Magnolia, introduced between 1780 and 1817
Magnolia fraseri	Ear-leaved Magnolia
Magnolia glauca	Glaucus or Swamp Magnolia, Sweet Bay
Magnolia grandiflora var. *lanceolata*	Exmouth Magnolia
Magnolia macrophylla	Big-leaf Magnolia
Magnolia X *soulangeana*	Saucer Magnolia
Mangolia X *thompsoniana*	Thompson's Magnolia
Magnolia tripetala	Umbrella Magnolia
Mahonia aquifolium	Oregon Holly-grape, named in 1822 for Bernard M'Mahon
Malus angustifolia	Narrow-leaved Crab, Southern Crabapple
Malus baccata	Siberian Crab Apple
Malus prunifolia	Siberian Crab
Malus spectabilis	Chinese Apple Tree
Melia azedarach *	Chinaberry, Pride of China, Bead Tree
Menispermum canadense	Canadian Moonseed
Morus alba	White Italian Mulberry
Morus multicaulis	Mulberry—During the era of the "silk mania," 1826–1841, more of these trees were probably sold than any other.

150 SHRUBS, TREES, AND VINES—1776–1850 (Continued)

Morus nigra	Black Mulberry
Morus rubra	Red Mulberry, American Mulberry
Myricaria germanica	German Tamarisk, False Tamarisk
Nandina domestica	Nandina, introduced in 1804
Ocimum minimum	Bush Basil—According to Bailey this is probably a small form of *O. Basilicum* which appears before 1700.
Ononis fruticosa	Shrubby Rest Harrow
Paeonia suffruticosa	Tree Peony, introduced in 1800
Paulownia tomentosa	Empress-tree—Not introduced until 1834. It is in trade at least by 1844.
Periploca graeca*	Virginian Silk Tree—Periploca is referred to in 1600s, but without scientific name.
Philadelphus inodorus	Scentless Mock-Orange
Phillyrea angustifolia	Phillyrea
Phillyrea latifolia	Phillyrea
Phillyrea latifolia var. *media*	Phillyrea
Physocarpus opulifolius	Nine-bark
Picea abies	Fir, Norway Spruce, introduced in the 1840s
Picea glauca	Fir, White Spruce
Picea mariana	Fir, Black Spruce
Picea orientalis	Oriental Spruce, introduced in 1837
Pieris floribunda	Mountain Andromeda, introduced between 1802 and 1814
Pinus cembra	Siberian Stone Pine, Swiss Stone Pine
Pinus flexilis	Limber Pine, not discovered until 1819 or 1820
Pinus mugo	Mugho Pine, Mountain Pine
Pinus pinaster	Cluster Pine, Pinaster
Pinus pinea	Stone Pine, Italian Stone Pine
Pinus resinosa	Pitch Pine—*P. resinosa* is Red Pine and Pitch Pine is *P. rigida*, according to Bailey.
Pinus sylvestris	Scotch Pine
Platanus orientalis*	Oriental Plane Tree
Polygala chamaebuxus	Box-leaved Milkwort
Populus alba	White Poplar
Populus angulata	Probably a hybrid between *P. balsamifera* and *P. nigra*
Populus candicans	Balm of Gilead
Populus heterophylla	Swamp Cottonwood, Various-leaved Poplar
Populus nigra	Black Poplar
Populus nigra var. *italica*	Lombardy Poplar, not introduced until 1784
Populus tremula	European Aspen
Populus tremuloides	Quaking Aspen
Prunus angustifolia	Narrow-leaved Cherry, Chickasaw Plum
Prunus glandulosa	Dwarf-flowering Almond, not introduced until 1835
Prunus lusitanica	Portugal Laurel
Prunus mahaleb	Perfumed Cherry, St. Lucie Cherry
Prunus padus	European Bird Cherry

Prunus persica, double flowered	Flowering Peach	151
Prunus pumila	Dwarf Canadian, Sand Cherry	
Prunus serrulata	Japanese Flowering Cherry	
Prunus spinosa	Blackthorn, Sloe	
Pseudotsuga menziesii	Douglas Fir	
Punica granatum fl. pl.	Double-flowering Pomegranate	
*Pyracantha coccinea**	Scarlet or Everlasting Firethorn	
Pyrus salicifolia	Willow-leaved Crab	
Quercus aegilops	Large Prickly-cupped Oak	
Quercus bicolor	Downy-leaved Chestnut Oak, Swamp White Oak	
Quercus cinerea	Upland Willow Oak, Blue Jack	
Quercus ilicifolia	Banister's Dwarf Oak, Bear or Scrub Oak	
Quercus imbricaria	Shingle Oak	
Quercus laevis	Sandy Red Oak	
Quercus laurifolia	Laurel-leaved Oak, Laurel Oak	
Quercus lyrata	Water White Oak, Overcup Oak, Swamp or Swamp Post Oak	
Quercus macrocarpa	Overcup White Oak, Burr Oak, Mossy Cup Oak	
Quercus montana	Mountain Chestnut Oak, Chestnut Oak, Rock Chestnut Oak	
Quercus muhlenbergii	Narrow-leaved Chestnut Oak, Yellow Chestnut Oak	
Quercus nigra	Carolina Water Oak, Water Oak	
Quercus palustris	Swamp Red Oak	
Quercus prinoides	Chinquapin Chestnut Oak, Chincapin Oak	
Quercus pumila	Dwarf Marsh Oak	
Quercus robur	English Oak	
Quercus stellata	Upland White Oak, Iron Oak, Post Oak	
Quercus velutina	Champlain Black Oak, Black Oak, Yellow-Bark Oak	
Rhamnus catharticus	Purging Buckthorn	
Rhamnus frangula	Berry-bearing Alder	
Rhododendron camtschaticum	Rhododendron Kamptschatka	
Rhododendron canadense	Canada Rhodora	
Rhododendron catawbiense	Catawba Rhododendron, found in 1796 and then brought into cultivation	
Rhododendron caucasicum	Mt. Caucasus Rhododendron	
Rhododendron chrysanthum	Dwarf Rhododendron	
Rhododendron dauricum	Dotted-leaved Rhododendron	
Rhododendron ferrugineum	Rusty-leaved Rhododendron	
Rhododendron hirsutum	Hairy Rhododendron	
Rhododendron indicum	Indian Azalea, introduced in 1838	
Rhododendron maximum	Rhododendron, Broad-leaved Mountain Laurel	
Rhodothamnus chamaecistus	Austrian Rhododendron	
Rhus chinensis	Chinese Sumac	
Rhus copallina	Lentiscus-leaved Sumac	
Rhus coriaria	Tanners Sumack	
Rhus glabra	Smooth Sumac	
Rhus radicans	Poison Vine, Ash, Poison Ivy	
*Rhus toxicodendron**	Poison Oak	
Rhus typhina	Stag's Horn	

SHRUBS, TREES, AND VINES—1776–1850 (Continued)

Rhus vernix	Varnish Tree, Poison Sumac, Swamp Sumac, Poison Dogwood
Ribes aureum	Golden Currant
Ribes cynobasti	Prickly-fruited Gooseberry
Rosa alba var. *fl. pl.*	Double-white Rose
Rosa arvensis	White Dog Rose
Rosa banksiae	Chinese Rose, introduced between 1780 and 1817
Rosa blanda	Hudson's Bay Rose
Rosa carolina	Carolina Rose, Pasture Rose
Rosa centifolia var. *muscosa*	Moss Province Rose
Rosa centifolia var. *parvifolia*	Small-leaved Cabbage Rose
Rosa chinensis	Pale China Rose
Rosa cinnamonea	Cinnamon Rose
Rosa foetida	Single Yellow Austrian Rose, Austrian Brier
Rosa foetida var. *persiana*	Double Yellow Austrian Rose, Persian Yellow Rose
Rose indica	Indian Rose
Rosa moschata var. *fl. pl.*	Double Musk Rose—This is a 1600s rose but now double.
Rosa multiflora	Many-flowered Rose
Rosa pendulina	Alpine Rose
Rosa pendulina var. *pyrenaica*	Pyrenean Rose
Rosa rubrifolia	Red-leaved Rose
Rosa rugosa	Wrinkled-leaved Rose
Rosa sempervirens	Evergreen Rose—The Evergreen Rose referred to in 1600s could be this one.
Rosa virginiana	Shining Leaved American Rose
Rubus odoratus	Flowering Raspberry
Rubus spectabilis	Salmon-berry
*Ruscus aculeatus**	Butchersbroom, Prickly Butcher's Broom
*Salix babylonica**	Babylonian Willow, Weeping Willow
Sambucus nigra	Common European Elder
Sambucus nigra var. *laciniata*	Parsley-leaved Elder
Sambucus pubens	Hairy Elder, American Red Elder
Sambucus racemosa	European Red-berried Elder
Skimmia japonica	Japanese Skimmia, introduced in 1838
Smilax bona-nox	Ciliated or Prickly-leaved Smilax, Saw Brier
Smilax lanceolata	Spear-leaved Smilax
Smilax laurifolia	Bay-leaved Smilax, False China Brier
Smilax rotundifolia	Canadian Round-leaved Smilax
Solanum dulcamara	Woody Nightshade, Bitter Sweet
*Sophora japonica**	Scholar Tree
Sophora japonica pendula	Weeping Scholar Tree
Sorbus americana	American Service or Roane Tree, Mountain Ash
Sorbus aucuparia	European Service Tree, European Mountain Ash Rowan
Sorbus hybrida	Bastard Service Tree
Spiraea cantoniensis	Reeve's Spiraea, introduced in 1824

Spiraea crenata	Hawthorn-leaved Spiraea
Spiraea hypericifolia	Hypericum-leaved Spiraea
Spiraea salicifolia	Willow-leaved Spiraea
Staphylea trifoliata	Three-leaved Bladder Nut, American Bladder Nut—Bladdernut is referred to in the 1600s but not given genus and species. It is almost certainly this one or *S. pinnata*.
*Stewartia malachondendron**	Stewartia
Styrax grandifolium	Great-leaved Storax Tree or Big-Leaf Snowbell
Symphoricarpos albus laevigatus	Snowberry
Symphoricarpos rivularis	Snowberry, not until after 1800
Tamarix gallica	French Tamarisk
Thuja orientalis	Chinese Arbor Vitae
Tilia tomentosa	White or Silver-leaved Linden
Ulmus americana var. *pendula*	American Drooping Elm
Ulmus carpinifolia	Smooth-leaved Elm
Ulmus carpinifolia var. *stricta*	Cornish Elm
Ulmus fulva	Red American Elm, Slippery Elm
Ulmus glabra	Scotch or Wych Elm
Ulmus hollandica	Dutch Elm
Ulmus parvifolia	Chinese Elm, introduced in 1794
Ulmus procera	English Elm
Ulmus pumila	Dwarf Elm
Vaccinium arboreum	Tree Huckleberry, Farkleberry or Sparkleberry
Vaccinium corymbosum	Cluster-flowered Huckle-berry, Highbush or Swamp Blueberry, Whortleberry
Vaccinium myrtillus	European Huckleberry, Bill-berry, Whortleberry
Vaccinium oxycoccos	European Cranberry, Bog-berry
Vaccinium stamineum	Green-twigged Huckle-berry, Deerberry
Viburnum alnifolium	Alder-leaved Viburnum, Hobble Bush, American Wayfaring Tree
Viburnum laevigatum	Cassioberry Bush
Viburnum nudum	Oval-leaved Viburnum, Smooth Withe Rod
Viburnum plicatum	Japanese Snowball, introduced in 1814
Viburnum tinus	Lauristinus
Viburnum tomentosum var. *sterile*	Japanese Snowball—Not too popular until Thomas Meehan's nursery began to specialize in this plant in 1853.
Vinca major	Large Periwinkle
Wisteria sinensis	Chinese Wisteria—Probably not much used until after 1825.
Xanthoriza simplicissima	Shrub Yellow Root
Yucca gloriosa	Mound Lily Yucca, Spanish Dagger
Zanthoxylum clava-herculis	Ash-leaved Tooth-ack Tree, Hercules Club

VEGETABLES AND FIELD CROPS—1776–1850

Agaricus campestris	Mushroom
Allium ascalonicum	Shallot

154 VEGETABLES AND FIELD CROPS—1776–1850 (Continued)

Allium scorodopnasum	Rocambole, Giant Garlic
Apium graveolens var. *rapaceum*	Celeriac, Turnep-rooted Celery
Arachis hypogoea	Ground Nut, Goober, Peanut
Armoracia rusticana	Horse Radish
Atriplex hortensis	Orach, English Lamb's-quarter—Two varieties: Large Green-leaved, Large Red-leaved.
Brassica oleracea var. *acephala* and other varieties	Kale, Borecole
Brassica oleracea var. *gemmifera*	Brussels Sprouts
Brassica oleracea var. *italica*	Italian Broccoli
Cichorium endivia	Green-curled, White-curled, or Broad Leaved Endive
Crambe maritima	Sea Kale, Cabbage
Cucumis anguria	Round Prickly Cucumber, India or Bur Gherkin
Ipomaea batatas	Sweet Potatoe
Lycopersicon esculentum	Tomatoes or Love-apple
Nasturtium officinale	Water Cress
Onyza sativa	Rice
Rumex scutatus	Round-leaved Sorrel
Scorzonera hispanica	Scorzonera, Black Salsify
Solanum melongena	Egg Plant
Tragapogon porrifolius	Salsafy, Vegetable Oyster
Vicia faba	Common Garden Bean—McMahon lists 14 varieties.

FRUITS AND NUTS—1776–1850

Anana comosus	Pineapple
Carica papaya	Papaya, Pawpaw—Also grown for ornamental purposes later, the first season for foliage
Citrus paradisi	Grapefruit—The only citrus fruits grown until post–Civil War were oranges and grapefruits
Citrus sinensis var.	Naval Orange, introduced just prior to Civil War
Cocos nucifera	Coconut
Mangifera indica	Mango

HERBS: AROMATIC, CULINARY, AND MEDICINAL—1776–1850

Achillea ageratum	Sweet Yarrow
Althea officinalis	Marsh Mallow
Anagalis arvensis	Pimpernel, Poor Man's Weatherglass
Apium graveolens	Smallage
Aristolochia serpentaria	Virginia Snake-root
Artemisia absinthium	Wormwood
Artemisia vulgaris	Common Mugwort
Chelidonium majus	Celandine
Chenepodium ambrosioides, probably	Wormseed, Goosefoot, Mexican Tea
Cnicus benedictus	Carduus Benedictus, Blessed Thistle
Cochlearia officinalis	Scurvy-grass
Eupatorium perfoliatum	Ague-weed, Thoroughwort, Common Boneset

Lithospermum officinale	Gromwell
Majorana onites	Pot Marjoram
Mandragora sp., probably	Mandrake
Marrubium vulgare	Horehound
Papaver somniferum	Opium Poppy
Rheum palmatum	Rhubarb, True Turkey
Ricinus communis	Castor-oil Nut, Palma Christi, Castor Bean
Satureja hortensis	Summer Savory, referred to before 1700, but not by species
Satureja montana	Winter Savory, probably grown in the 1600s as well
Spigelia marilandica	Carolina Pink-root
Stachys officinalis	Wood Betony, Woundwort
Thymus vulgaris	Common Thyme
Trigonella foenum graecum	Fenugreek
Urtica dioica	**Stinging Nettle**
Valerianella olitoria	Corn-sallad

FLOWERS—1850–1900

Acanthus sp.	Bear's Breech
Achillea fillipendulina	Fernleaf Yarrow
Achillea millefolium rosea	Yarrow or Milfoil variety
*Achillea ptarmica, fl. pl.**	Sneezewort
Achillea tomentosa	Downy Yarrow, Wooly Yarrow
Aconitum autumnale	Autumn Monk's-hood
Acorus calamus	Sweet Flag
*Adonis vernalis**	Spring Adonis
Agapanthus africanus	African-Lily, Lily-of-the-Nile
Ailanthus altissima	Tree-of-heaven—Keep a young one pruned to the roots every spring to have very large foliage for garden. So also with *Paulownia*. Henderson.
Ajuga reptans var. *alba*	Carpet Bugle, Bugle-weed
Alisma sp.	Water Plantain
Aloe sp.	Aloe
Alternanthera bettzickiana	Alternanthera
Althea officinalis	Swamp Mallow, Marsh-Mallow
*Althea rosea**	Hollyhock
Allyssum repens var. *wierzbickii*	Alyssum
Alyssum saxatile	Golden Tuft, Gold-dust, Basket-of-gold, Rock Madwort
Alyssum saxatile var. *compactum*	Dwarf Golden Tuft
Amaranthus hybridus var. *hypochondriacus*	Prince's Feather
Amaranthus tricolor var. *salicifolius**	Fountain Plant
Amorphophallus campanulatus or *rivieri*	Stanley's Wash-Tub. *A. rivieri* is now *Hydrosome rivieri*, Devil's Tongue, Snake Palm
Anemone apennina	Anemone
Anemone blanda	Windflower
Anemone caroliniana	Windflower
Anemone hupehensis japonica	Autumn Flowering Anemone

FLOWERS—1850–1900 (Continued)

Anemone japonica	Japanese Anemone
Anemone nemorosa	European Wood Anemone
Anemone patens var. *nuttalliana*	Windflower, Pasque-flower
Anemone pulsatilla	European Pasque-flower, Pasque-flower
Anemone quinquefolia	Wood Anemone
Anemone sylvestris	Snowdrop Wind-flower
Anthemis tinctoria	Yellow Chamomile, Golden Marguerite
Anthericum liliago	St. Bernard's Lily
Antirrhinum glutinosum	Snapdragon
Aquilegia caerulea	Rocky Mountain Columbine
Aquilegia canadensis*	Canada Columbine
Aquilegia chrysantha	Golden or Golden-spurred Columbine, "probably the best because it produces golden-yellow flowers all summer"
Aquilegia sibirica	Siberian Columbine
Aquilegia vulgaris var. *nivea*	Munstead Giant, Munsteads White Columbine
Arabis alpina	Alpine Rock Cress
Arenaria verna	Spring Sandwort
Armeria maritima var. *elongata**	Sea Pink, Thrift
Aruncus sylvester*	Goat's Beard
Arundo donax	Green-leaved Bamboo, Giant Reed
Asclepias tuberosa*	Butterfly Weed, Swallow-wort
Asparagus sprengeri	Emerald Fern, Emerald-feather
Asperula odorata	Common Woodruff, Sweet Woodruff
Asphodelus luteus*	Asphodel, King's Spear
Aster amellus var. *bessarabicus*	Russian Starwort, Italian Aster
Aster bigelovii	Aster
Aster novae-angliae*	New England Aster
Aster novae-angliae var. *roseus*, probably	New England Aster variety
Aster ptarmicoides	White Upland Aster
Aster shortii	Aster
Astilbe japonica	Spiraea (of florists)
Aubrieta sp.	Half dozen or more species
Aubrieta leichtlinii	Leichtlinii (a trade name) is probably a horticultural variant or intervarietal hybrid of *A. deltoidea*.
Baptisia australis	Blue False Indigo
Bergenia cordifolia	Heart-leaved Saxifrage
Beta vulgaris var. *cicla*	Ornamental-leaved Beets, Leaf-Beet
Bulbocodium vernum	Spring Meadow Saffron
Caladium bicolor	Caladium
Calla palustris	Water Arum
Callirhoe involucrata	Crimson Mallow, Poppy-mallow
Campanula carpatica*	Carpet Bell-flower
Campanula isophylla var. *alba*	Bellflower
Campanula medium*	Canterbury Bells, singles and doubles
Campanula medium var. *calycanthema*	Cup-and-Saucer
Campanula rotundifolia	Harebell

*Carica papaya**	Papaya, Pawpaw, first season for foliage
*Cassia marilandica**	American Senna, Wild Senna
Cerastium biebersteinii	Mouse Ear
Cerastium tomentosum	Snow-in-summer
Ceratostigma plumbaginoides	Leadwort
Chionodoxa lucilia	Glory-of-the-snow
Chrysanthemum sp.*	Japanese and Chinese Chrysanthemums
Chrysanthemum lacustre	Portuguese Chrysanthemum, "white moon-penny daisies"
Chrysanthemum maximum	Max Chrysanthemums or Daisy—". . . Known in many forms, as King Edward VII, Chrysanthemum daisy, Shasta daisy, Glory of the Wayside, . . ." Parsons.
Chrysanthemum uliginosum	Giant Daisy, "white moon-penny daisies"
Clematis heracleaefolia var. *davidiana*	Clematis
*Clematis integrifolia**	Virgin's Bower
Clematis recta	Upright Virgin's Bower
Cobaea scandens	Monastery-Bells, Mexican Ivy, Cup-and-Saucer Vine
Codiaeum variegatum var. *pictum*	Croton, many forms
*Colchicum autumnale**	Autumn Crocus
*Convallaria majalis**	Lily-of-the-valley
Coreopsis sp.	Golden Coreopsis, perhaps *C. drummondii*, Golden Wave
*Coreopsis lanceolata**	Tickseed
Cortaderia selloana	Pampas Grass
Corydalis nobilis	Corydalis
Crinum longifolium, probably	Crinum
Crocus susianus	Cloth-of-gold Crocus
*Crocus vernus**	Crocus
Crocus versicolor	Crocus
Crucianella stylosa	Crosswort
Cymbalaria muralis	Kenilworth Ivy
Cyperus alternifolius	Umbrella Plant
Cyperus papyrus	Papyrus
Cypripedium sp.*	Moccasin Flower
Dahlia sp.	Dahlias, especially singles which "have been deservedly increasing in reputation of late" Parsons.
Datura humilis flava, fl. pl.	A horticultural variety of *D. metel* "large, yellow, sweet-scented flowers"
*Datura metel**	Datura, Downy Thorn Apple, Horn-of-Plenty
Datura metel alba plena	Datura variety
Datura inoxia quinquecuspida	Downy Thorn Apple, Indian Apple, Angel's Trumpet, Tolguacha
Delphinium cheilanthum var. *formosum*	Beautiful Larkspur, Garland Larkspur
*Delphinium elatum**	Tall Larkspur, Candle or Bee Larkspur
Delphinium grandiflorum	Bouquet Larkspur, Double-flowering Larkspur
Delphinium nudicaule	Red Larkspur
*Dianthus barbatus**	Sweet-william

*Dianthus deltoides**	Maiden's Pink
Dianthus gratianopolitanus	Cheddar Pinks
*Dianthus plumarius**	Garden Pink, Cushion Pink, Cottage Pink
Dicentra eximia	Plumy Bleeding-heart
Dicentra spectabilis	Bleeding Heart
*Dictamnus albus**	Gas Plant, Dittany, Fraxinella, Burning Bush
*Digitalis purpurea**	Foxglove
Digitalis purpurea var. *gloxiniae-flora*	Gloxinia-flowered Foxglove
*Dodecatheon meadia**	American Cowslip, Shooting Star
Dolichos lablab, probably*	Hyacinth Bean, Bonavist
Dracocephalum ruyschiana	Hyssop-leaved Dragon's-head
Eichornia crassipes	Water-hyacinth
*Epimedium grandiflorum**	Barrenwort, especially var. alba
*Eranthis hyemalis**	Winter Aconite
Erianthus ravennae	Plume-grass, Ravenna-grass
Erinus alpinus var. *hirsutus*	Erinus
*Eryngium alpinum**	Alpine Eryngium
Eucalyptus globulus	Blue Gum, first season for foliage
Euphorbia corollata	Flowering Spurge
Ferns	Especially native species in naturalistic settings
Ferula communis	Giant Fennel
Ficus elastica	Rubber Plant
Filipendula hexapetala var. *fl.pl.* *	Dropwort, "old and favorite plant"
Filipendula palmata	Meadowsweet
Filipendula rubra var. *venusta*	Queen of the Prairies
Filipendula ulmaria	Meadow-sweet, Queen of the Meadow
Gaillardia aristata	Gaillardia—Have been much improved recently. Parsons
Galanthus elwesii	Giant Snowdrop
*Galanthus nivalis**	Snowdrop
Gaultonia candicans	Giant Summer Hyacinth
Gaura lindheimeri	Gaura
*Gentiana acaulis**	Stemless Gentian
Gentiana andrewsii	Closed Gentian
Geranium sanguineum	Blood-red Geranium
Gillenia trifoliata	Bowman's Root, Indian Physic
Grevillea robusta	Silk Oak, first season for foliage
Gunnera manicata	Gunnera
Gypsophila paniculata	Baby's-Breath
Helenium hoopesii	Sneezeweed
Helianthus sp.*	Double Perennial Sunflower
Helianthus maximilianii	Maximilian Sunflower
Helianthus salicifolius	Graceful Sunflower
*Helleborus niger**	Christmas Rose
Helleborus niger altifolius	One of best varieties
Helonias bullata	Swamp-Pink
*Hemerocallis flava**	Day Lily

Hemerocallis thunbergii	Late Yellow Daylily
*Hepatica americana**	Liver-leaf
*Hesperis matronalis**	Double Rocket, double purple and double white
Hibiscus lasiocarpos var. *californicus*	Mallow, Giant Mallow
*Hibiscus moscheutos**	Marsh Rose-mallow
Hosta caerulea	Blue Plantain
Hosta plantaginea	Plantain Lily, Fragrant Plantain, Day Lily
Hosta sieboldii	Seersucker, Plantain Lily
*Houstonia coerulea**	Bluets
Humea elegans	Humea
*Hyacinthus orientalis**	Many varieties
Hydrocleys nymphoides	Water Poppies
Iberis corifolia	Corris-leaved Perennial Candy Tuft
Iberis gibraltica	Gibraltar Candytuft
*Ipomaea purpurea**	Morning Glory
*Iris cristata**	Crested Iris
*Iris germanica**	German Iris—". . . by hybridization fine varieties with a great range of beautiful combinations of color have been secured."
Iris germanica var. *florentina**	Florentine Iris, Orris Root
Iris iberica	Chalcedonian Iris
Iris kaempferi	Japanese Iris
Iris orientalis	Iris
*Iris pumila**	Iris
Iris reticulata	Golden Netted Iris
*Iris sibirica**	Siberian Iris
Iris verna	Dwarf Iris
Kniphofia corallina	This is hybrid between *K. macowanii* and *K. uvaria*.
Kniphofia uvaria	Tritoma, Kniphofia, Red-hot Poker Plant, Torch Lily
Kniphofia uvaria var. *grandiflora*	Tritoma Variety
*Lathyrus latifolius**	Everlasting Pea
Leontopodium alpinum	Edelweiss
*Leucojum vernum**	Spring Snowflake
Liatris pycnostachya	Kansas Gay-feather
*Liatris spicata**	Button Snakeroot, Blazing Star, Gay Feather
Ligularia japonica	Groundsel
Lilium auratum	Goldband Lily
*Lilium canadense**	Meadow Lily
Lilium canadense var. *coccineum*	"Flowers brick-red with a yellow, spotted throat."
*Lilium candidum**	Madonna Lily
Lilium dauricum var. *venustum* form *batemanniae*	Lily
Lilium pardalinum	Leopard Lily
Lilium parryi	Lemon Lily
*Lilium pomponium**	Pomponian Lily, Lesser Turks-cap Lily
Lilium pyrenaicum	Yellow Turban Lily, Yellow Turks-cap
Lilium speciosum	Showy Japanese Lily
*Lilium superbum**	Turk's-cap Lily
Lilium tigrinum	Tiger Lily

160 FLOWERS—1850–1900 (Continued)

Lilium tigrinum var. *splendens*	Tiger Lily
Limonium latifolium	Woundwort
Lindheimera texana	Star Daisy
Linum perenne*	Perennial Flax
Lobelia cardinalis*	Cardinal Flower
Lotus corniculatus	Bird's-Foot Trefoil
Lupinus sp.*	Hardy Lupines
Lychnis chalcedonica*	Scarlet Lychnis, Maltese Cross—"It has been neglected for much less showy summer flowers."—Parsons
Lychnis chalcedonica, fl. pl.	Double Scarlet Lychnis
Lychnis viscaria var. *splendens*	German Catchfly
Lycoris squamigera	Hall's Amaryllis
Lysimachia sp.*	Loosestrife
Lythrum salicaria*	Purple Loosestrife
Macleaya cordata	Plume Poppy
Malva alcea	Garden Mallow
Malva moschata alba	Musk Mallow
Miscanthus sinensis var. *gracillimus*	Eulalia variety
Miscanthus sinensis var. *variegatus*	Eulalia variety
Miscanthus, probably *sinensis* var. *zebrinus*	Zebra Grass
Mitchella repens	Partridge-berry
Monarda didyma*	Bee Balm, Oswego Tea
Muscari sp.*	Grape Hyacinths
Narcissus imcomparabilis	Many forms
Narcissus odorus*	Campernelle Jonquil
Narcissus poeticus*	Poet's Narcissus, Pheasant's Eye
Narcissus pseudo-narcissus*	Daffodil or Daffodowndilly
Narcissus pseudo-narcissus, form bicolor*	Two-coloured Narcissus
Narcissus pseudo-narcissus, form maximus	Daffodil
Narcissus tazetta, form bicolor*	Two-coloured Narcissus
Narcissus triandrus var. *cernuus*	Angel's Tears
Nelumbium nelumbo	East Indian Lotus
Nelumbium pentapetalum*	Yellow Lotus
Nepeta hederacea*	Ground Ivy, Gill-over-the-ground, Field Balm
Nicotiana alata var. *grandiflora*	Nicotiana
Nierembergia rivularis	White-cup
Nymphaea alba var. *candidissima**	European White Water Lily Variety
Nymphaea capensis var. *zanzibarensis azurea*	Cape Blue Water Lily cultivar
Nymphaea capensis var. *zanzibarensis rosea*	Cape Blue Water Lily cultivar
Nymphaea X *devoniensis*	Water Lily
Nymphaea lotus	Egyptian Sacred Lotus, White Lotus of Egypt
Nymphaea odorata var. *rosea**	Fragrant Water Lily, Cape Cod Pink Lily
Nymphaea tetragona	Pygmy Water-Lily
Nymphoides indicum	Water Snowflake
Oenothera sp.*	Tall Evening Primrose

Oenothera missouriensis	Evening Primrose
Oenothera speciosa	Evening Primrose
Opuntia sp.	Prickly Pear, Indian Fig Type
Opuntia compressa	Western Prickly Pear
Orontium aquaticum	Golden Club
Osmunda regalis	Royal Fern
Paeonia sp.*	Peony
Paeonia tenuifolia, fl. pl. *	Peony
Papaver sp.*	Annual Poppies
Papaver bracteatum	Poppy
Papaver orientale *	Oriental Poppy
Papaver nudicaule var. *croceum*	Iceland Poppy
Paradisea liliastrum	St. Bruno's Lily
Paulownia tomentosa	Royal Paulownia, Empress Tree—Henderson recommends keeping a young tree pruned back to the roots each spring so as to have very attractive, large foliage for the garden.
Pelargonium peltatum	Ivy-leaved Geranium
Pelargonium zonale	Horseshoe Geranium
Pennisetum ruppellii	Fountain Grass
Pennisetum villosum	Grass
Penstemon coboea	Beard Tongue
Penstemon torreyi	Beard Tongue
Perilla frutescens var. *crispa*	Perilla
Petalostemum decumbens	Prairie Clover
Petunia hybrida	Common Garden Petunia
Phalaris arundinacea var. *picta*	Ribbon Grass
Phlox carolina	"No garden would, of course, be complete without its peonies and fall phloxes." Parsons.
Phlox decussata	Summer Perennial Phlox—Decussata is a name applied to horticultural forms of *phlox paniculata**, *P. maculata, P. suffruticosa*. Bailey.
Phlox nivalis var. *alba*	Trailing Phlox, Fine-leaved Phlox
Phlox procumbens	Thought to be a cross between *P. stolonifera* and *P. subulata*.
Phlox stellaria	Starry Phlox
Phlox subulata *	Ground Phlox, Moss Pink
Phyllostachys sp.	Bamboo—*Phyllostachys niger henonis, P. nigra* and *P. viridi-glaucescens* are especially hardy.
Piqueria trinervia var. *variegata*	Stevia
Platycodon grandiflorum	Large Bell-flower, Balloon Flower
Polygonatum sp.*	Solomon's Seal
Primula sp.*	Hardy Primulas
Primula japonica	Japanese Primrose
Primula vulgaris *	Common, Wild English Primrose—S. Parsons recommends this but says it is seldom grown.
Ranunculus speciosus, fl. pl.	Bachelor's-button, Creeping Buttercup
Rheum palmatum	Giant Rhubarb

Ricinus communis *	Castor-oil Plant
Rubus odoratus	Purple-flowering Raspberry—"old well-known plant of the highest excellence." Parsons.
Rudbeckia laciniata var. *hortensia*	Coneflower, Golden Glow. Flowers double
Rudbeckia maxima	Large Cone-flower
Salvia pratensis	Meadow-sage
Sanguinaria canadensis *	Bloodroot
Saponaria ocymoides *	Basil-leaved Soapwort
Sarracenia sp.*	Pitcher Plants
Saxifraga sp.*	Saxifrage, Rockfoil
Saxifraga longifolia	Saxifrage, Rockfoil
Scabiosa caucasica	Scabious, Mourning Bridge, Pincushion-flower
Scilla sp.*	Scilla
Sedum acre	Common Stone-crop
Sedum sieboldii	October Daphne, October Plant
Sedum spectabile	Sedum
Sempervivum arachnoideum *	Cobweb House Leek
Sempervivum calcareum	Houseleek
Sempervivum tectorum	Common House-leek, Roof Houseleek, Hen-and-chickens, Old-man-and-woman
Senecio cineraria var. *candidissimus*	Cineraria (White leaved)
Silene caroliniana *	Wild Pink, Pennsylvania Catchfly
Silene virginica *	Fire Pink
Silphium laciniatum *	Compass Plant
Solidago canadensis	Goldenrod
Solidago rigida	Goldenrod
Solidago shortii	Goldenrod
Stipa pennata	Spear Grass, Feather Grass
Stokesia laevis *	Stoke's Aster
Symplocarpus foetidus	Skunk Cabbage
Tetrapanax papyriferum	Rice-Paper Plant
Thalictrum glaucum	Meadow-rue—"fine large yellow-flowered sort with handsome leaves which grow three to five feet high." Parsons.
Thymus serpyllum var. *aureus*, also var. *argenteus* and *variegatus*	Variegated Thyme, Mother-of-thyme, Creeping Thyme
Tradescantia virginica *	Spiderwort
Trillium sp.*	Trillium
Trollius europaeus	European Globe Flower
Tropaeolum majus *	Nasturtium
Tropaeolum majus probably var. *burpeei*	Double Nasturtium, Golden Gleam Nasturtium
Tulipa sp.*	Tulips
Tunica saxifraga	Rock Tunica
Typha latifolia *	Cat-tails
Verbascum sp.*	Verbascum, Mullein
Verbascum olympicum	Mullein
Verbena hortensis *	Garden Verbena

Vernonia noveboracensis	New York Iron-weed
Veronica gentianoides	Gentian Leaved Speedwell
Veronica longifolia var. *subsessilis*	Best of the Speedwells
Veronica spuria	"Better than Gentianoides." Parsons.
*Vinca minor**	Trailing Vinca
Viola cornuta	Horned Violet
*Viola pedata**	Bird's-foot Violet
Xeriphyllum asphodeloides	Turkey's Beard
*Yucca filamentosa**	Yucca
Zantedeschia sp.	Calla
Zea mays var. *curarua* and var. *japonica*	Corn for ornamentation

BEDDING PLANTS—1850–1900

Abutilon hybridum var. *souvenir de bonn*	Abutilon, variegated-leaved
Acalypha wilkesiana vr. *macrophylla*	Copper-leaf
Acalypha wilkesiana var. *musaica*	Copper-leaf, Giant Redleaf
Agave americana	Century Plant, for pots and bedding
Ageratum sp.	Dwarf Blue Ageratum
Alternanthera amoena	Telanthera, Parrotleaf, Shoofly Joyweed
Alternanthera bettzickiana	Telanthera, Calico Plant
Alternanthera bettzickiana var. *aurea*	Calico Plant variety
Alternanthera bettzickiana var. *aurea nana*	Calico Plant variety
Alternanthera versicolor	Copper Alternanthera
Begonia semperflorens	Begonia Vernon
Begonia tuberhybrida	Tuberous Begonia
Canna ehmannii now C. *generalis*	Canna
Canna ehemannii X. *glauca* and others now included in C. *generalis*	Dwarf French Canna
Canna indica	Indian Shot, many varieties
Centaurea gymnocarpa	Dusty Miller
Chrysanthemum sp.*	Daisies
Chrysanthemum parthenium var. *aureum*	Feverfew, Golden Feather
Coleus sp.	Varieties of diverse sorts
Coleus blumei var. *golden bedder*	Coleus hybrid
Coleus blumei var. *kirkpatrick*	Coleus hybrid
Coleus blumei var. *vershaffeltii*	Butterfly coleus
Colocasia esculenta	Elephant Ear, Taro, Eddo, Dasheen
Cordyline indivisa	Cordyline
Cuphea platycentra	Cigar Flower
Echeveria gibbiflora var. *metallica*	Hen-and-Chickens
Echeveria secunda var. *glauca*	Hen-and-Chickens
Gladiolus hortulanus	Gladiolus, Sword Lily, Garden Gladioli, Hortulan
Iresine sp.	Bloodleaf
Lantana camara var. *hybrida*	Dwarf Lantana
Lobelia erinus	Edging Lobelia
*Lobularia maritima**	Sweet Alyssum
Lobularia maritima (variegated)	Alyssum, variegated
Musa ensete	Banana Plant, Abyssinian Banana

164   BEDDING PLANTS—1850–1900 (Continued)

Nierembergia sp.	Cupflower
Oxalis corniculata var. *atropurpurea*	Purple Creeping Oxalis, Purple Creeping Lady's Sorrel
Pelargonium sp.	Geranium, doubles and singles
Pelargonium sp.	Silver-leaved Geranium
Pelargonium zonale	Horseshoe Geranium
Piqueria trinervia	Stevia
*Ricinus communis**	Castor-oil Plant
Salvia splendens	Scarlet Salvia
*Santolina chamaecyparissus**	Lavender-cotton
Sedum acre	Common Stone-crop
Senecio leucostachys	Centauria, Dusty Miller
Solanum warscewiczii, now *S. hispidum*	Devil's Fig
Thymus serpyllum var. *variegatus*	Variegated Thyme
*Tropaeolum majus**	Garden Nasturtium
Tulipa gesneriana	Tulip varieties: La Belle Alliance, excellent red; Artus, excellent red; Pottebaker, white; Yellow Prince, yellow; Canary Bird, yellow
Tulipa suaveolens	Duc Van Tholl Tulip, Red-dwarf
Vinca rosea	Madascagar Periwinkle
Viola tricolor var. *hortensis*	Pansies

SHRUBS, TREES, AND VINES—1850–1900

Abies alba var. *compacta*	Dwarf Silver Fir
Abies alba var. *pendula*	Weeping Silver Fir
Abies balsamea var. *hudsonia*	Dwarf Hudson's Bay Fir
Abies cephalonica	Greek Fir
Abies cilicica	Cilician Fir
Abies concolor	White Fir
Abies lasiocarpa	Alpine Fir
Abies nobilis	Noble Fir
Abies nordmannia	Nordmann Fir
Abies sibirica	Siberian Silver Fir
Acanthopanax sieboldianus	Five-leaf Aralia
Acer cappadocicum	Coliseum Maple
Acer cappadocicum var. *rubrum*	Red Coliseum Maple
Acer japonicum	Fullmoon Maple, "fine red flowers"
Acer japonicum aureum	Yellow Leaves
*Acer palmatum**	Japanese Maple, there are many varieties
Acer palmatum ornatum	Spider-leaf Japanese Maple
Acer palmatum sanguineum	Scarlet Japanese Maple
*Acer pennsylvanicum**	Striped Maple, Moosewood
*Acer platanoides**	Norway Maple
Acer platanoides 'lorbergii'	Norway Maple Variety
Acer platanoides 'schwedleri'	Swedler Maple
*Acer pseudo-platanus**	Sycamore Maple

Acer pseudo-platanus var. *leopoldii* — Sycamore Maple variety
Acer pseudo-platanus var. *purpureum* — Sycamore Maple variety; also many other varieties: Silver Variegated, Golden Tinged, Golden, Striped, etc.

*Acer rubrum** — Red, Scarlet, Swamp Maple
Acer rufinerve — Red-veined Maple
Acokanthera spectabilis — Winter Sweet
Actinidia chinensis — China Gooseberry
*Adlumia fungosa** — Mountain Fringe, Climbing Fumitory, Allegheny Vine

Aesculus carnea — Red-flowering Horse Chestnut, "perhaps finest of all"

*Aesculus hippocastanum** — Horse Chestnut
Aesculus parviflora — Bottlebrush Buckeye, Dwarf Horse Chestnut
*Akebia quinata** — Five-leaf Akebia, not introduced until 1845
*Albizzia julibrissin** — Virginia Silk
Albizzia lophantha — Plume Albizia
Alnus firma — Japan Alder
Alnus glutinosa var. *imperialis* — Cut-leaved Alder, Black Alder
Amorpha sp.* — False Indigo, "small purplish flowers in dense terminal flattish clusters during early summer"

Ampelopsis brevipedunculata — Porcelain Ampelopsis
*Aralia elata** — Japanese Angelica Tree
*Aralia spinosa** — Hercules Club
Areca sp. — Feather-palm
*Aristolochia durior** — Dutchman's Pipe
Aucuba japonica — Japanese Aucuba
Berberis thunbergii — Japanese Barberry
Berberis thunbergii var. *atropurpurea* — Purple Barberry, Japanese Barberry
*Betula lenta** — Black Birch
*Betula lutea** — Yellow Birch
*Betula papyrifera** — White Birch, Canoe or Paper Birch
*Betula pendula** — Common European Birch, European White Birch, Weeping Birch

Betula pendula var. *purpurea* — Purple European Birch
Bougainvillea glabra — Bougainvillea, Paper Flower
Bougainvillea spectabilis — Bougainvillea
Buddleja davidii — Common Buddleia, Summer Lilac, introduced about 1890

Buxus microphylla — Little-leaf Box
Buxus sempervirens var. *arborescens* — Tree Box
Buxus sempervirens var. *suffruticosa* or another dwarf form* — Dwarf Box

Callicarpa dichotoma — Beauty-berry
Callicarpa japonica — Japanese Beauty-berry
Calycanthus fertilis var. *ferax* — Sweet-scented Shrub, Sweet Shrub
*Calycanthus floridus** — Sweet-scented Shrub, Carolina Allspice
Campsis grandiflora — Chinese Trumpet-creeper
*Campsis radicans** — Trumpet Creeper

Carnegiea gigantea	Sahuaro or Giant Cactus
Carpenteria californica	Tree Anemone
*Carpinus betulus**	European Hornbeam
*Carpinus caroliniana**	American Hornbeam
Caryota sp.	Fish-tail Palm
*Castanea dentata**	American Chestnut
*Catalpa bignonioides**	Southern Catalpa, Common Catalpa, Indian Bean
Catalpa bignonioides var. *aurea*	Golden Catalpa
Catalpa bignonioides var. *nana*	Dwarf Catalpa—*Catalpa bignonioides* var. *nana* "is the C. Bungii of horticulturists."
Cedrela sinensis	Chinese Toon
*Cedrus atlantica**	Atlas Cedar
*Cedrus libani**	Cedar of Lebanon
Celastrus orbiculatus	Asiatic Bittersweet Vine
*Celastrus scandens**	Bitter-sweet
Cercidiphyllum japonicum	Katsura-tree
Cercis chinensis	Chinese Redbud, Japan Judas Tree
*Cercis siliquastrum**	Japan Judas Tree, Judas Tree
Chaenomeles japonica	Dwarf Japanese Quince
*Chaenomeles lagenaria**	Japanese Quince, Flowering Quince
Chamaecyparis obtusa	Hinoki False Cypress
Chamaecyparis pisifera	Sawara False Cypress, Sawara Cypress
Chamaecyparis pisifera aurea	Golden Sawara False Cypress
Chamaecyparis pisifera filifera pendula	Sawara Cypress cultivar
Chamaecyparis pisifera var. *plumosa*	Sawara Cypress cultivar
Chamaecyparis pisifera squarrosa	Moss Sawara False Cypress
Chionanthus retusus	Fringe Tree
*Chionanthus virginica**	White Fringe Tree
*Cladrastis lutea**	American Yellow-wood
Clematis apiifolia	Clematis
Clematis flammula	Sweet-scented Clematis
Clematis florida	Cream Clematis—Hybrids: 'Belle of Woking,' double silver gray (1885); 'Duchess of Edinburgh,' double white (1877).
Clematis X *jackmanii*	Jackman Clematis—"perhaps the best." Parsons.
Clematis X *jackmanii* hybrids	Gypsy Queen, Madame Edouard Andre, Mrs. Cholmondeley, introduced before 1900
Clematis X *jouiniana*	Jouin Clematis
Clematis lanuginosa	Ningpo Clematis
Clematis lanuginosa hybrids	Perle d' Azur, Lady Caroline Neville, Lord Neville, Romona, W. E. Gladstone, introduced before 1890
Clematis lawsoniana var. *henryi*	Henry Clematis
Clematis paniculata	Sweet Autumn Clematis
Clematis paniculata var. *dioscoreifolia*	Clematis
Clematis patens	Lilac Clematis—Hybrids: 'Sir Garnet Wolseley' (1880), 'Edouard Desfosse' (1877).
Clematis tangutica	Golden Clematis, introduced in 1890

*Clematis virginiana**	Virgin's Bower
Clematis viticella hybrids	'Ascotiensis' (1880), 'Ville de Lyon' (1900), 'Kermesiana' (1883)
Clerodendron bungei	Rose Glory-bower
Clerodendrum trichotomum	Harlequin Glory-bower
*Clethra alnifolia**	Sweet Pepper Bush
Colutea sp.*	Bladder Senna
Cornus alba var. *sibirica*	Red-twigged Dogwood
*Cornus florida**	White-flowering Dogwood
Cornus florida pendula	Pendulous White-flowering Dogwood
*Cornus florida rubra**	Pink Dogwood
Cornus kousa	Kousa or Japanese Dogwood
Cornus kousa (variegated)	Grown in this country before the species itself
Corylus maxima purpurea	Purple Hazelnut, Filbert
*Cotinus coggygria**	Purple Fringe
Cotoneaster buxifolia	According to Bailey, material usually cultivated under this name is *C. rotundifolia* var. *lanata*
Cotoneaster horizontalis	Rock-spray, not used until after 1880
*Crataegus crus-galli**	Cock-spur Thorn
Cryptomeria japonica	Cryptomeria
Cryptomeria japonica elegans	Plume Cryptomeria
Cryptomeria japonica forma *variegata*	Cryptomeria
Cycas revoluta	Sago Palm
Cytisus praecox	Warminster Broom
*Cytisus scoparia**	Scotch Broom
Dalea spinosa	Smoke-tree
*Daphne cneorum**	Rose Daphne
Daphne genkwa	Daphne, Japan Daphne—Parsons wrote in 1891, "One of the more recent valuable introductions from Japan."
*Daphne mezereum**	Daphne, Mezereum
Deutzia gracilis	Slender Deutzia
Deutzia scabra fortunei	Large-white-flowered Deutzia
Deutzia scabra plena	Double-flowered Deutzia
Dioscorea batatas	Cinnamon Vine or Chinese Yam
Diospyros kaki	Japanese Persimmon or Kaki
*Diospyros virginiana**	American Persimmon
Dracaena draco	Dragon Tree
*Elaeagnus angustifolia**	Russian Olive
Elaeagnus multiflora	Cherry Elaeagnus, Gumi
Enkianthus campanulatus	Redvein Enkianthus
Erica carnea	Spring Heath
Euonymus alatus	Winged Euonymus
*Euonymus europaeus**	European Euonymus, Spindle Tree
Euonymus fortunei vegetus	Evergreen Bittersweet
Euonymus kiautschovica	Spreading Euonymus
*Euonymus latifolius**	Broadleaf Euonymus
*Exochorda racemosa**	Pearl Bush
*Fagus grandifolia**	American Beech

*Fagus sylvatica**	European Beech
Fagus sylvatica var. *atropunicea*	Purple Beech
Fagus sylvatica pendula	Weeping European Beech, Weeping Beech
Forsythia suspensa	Weeping Forsythia
Forsythia suspensa fortunii	Forsythia, Golden-bells
Forsythia viridissima	Forsythia, Golden-bells
*Fothergilla gardenii**	Dwarf Fothergilla
*Fraxinus excelsior**	European Ash
Fremontia californica	Flannel-bush
Garrya sp.	Silk-Tassel Bush
Genista tinctoria	Dyer's Greenweed
*Ginkgo biloba**	Ginkgo
Ginkgo biloba form *variegata*	Ginkgo variety
*Gleditsia tricanthos**	Honey Locust
Glyptostrobus pensilis	Chinese Cypress
*Gymnocladus dioicus**	Kentucky Coffee Tree
*Halesia carolina**	Snowdrop Tree, Silver-bell
*Halesia diptera**	Two-winged Snowdrop Tree
Hamamelis mollis	Chinese Witch-hazel
*Hamamelis virginiana**	Witch Hazel
Hibiscus rosasinensis	Chinese Hibiscus
*Hibiscus syriacus**	Althea
*Hibiscus syriacus fl. pl.**	Double Flowering Althea
Holocantha emoryi	Crucifixion-thorn
Holodiscus discolor var. *ariaefolius*	Rock-spirea
Hydrangea macrophylla var. *otaska*	House Hydrangea
Hydrangea paniculata grandiflora	Peegee Hydrangea
Hydrangea petiolaris	Climbing Hydrangea
Hydrangea quercifolia	Oak-leaved Hydrangea
Hypericum patulum	St. John's-wort
Ilex cornuta	Chinese Holly
*Ilex crenata**	Japanese Holly
*Ilex opaca**	American Holly
*Ilex verticillata**	Black Alder, Winterberry
*Itea virginica**	Virginian Willow, Sweet Spire
Jasminum nudiflorum	Jasmine
Juglans californica	California Black Walnut
Juniperus communis var. *depressa*	Canadian Juniper
Juniperus communis var. *hibernica*	Irish Juniper
Juniperus formosana	Weeping Juniper
Juniperus horizontalis	Creeping Juniper
Juniperus procumbens	Procumbent Juniper
*Juniperus sabina**	Savin Juniper
Juniperus sabina var. *tamariscifolia*	Tamarix Savin
Juniperus squamata	Himalayan Juniper
*Juniperus virginiana**	Red Cedar
Juniperus virginiana glauca	Silver Red Cedar

Juniperus virginiana pendula	Weeping Red Cedar
Juniperus virginiana var. *venusta*	Red Cedar Variety
*Kalmia latifolia**	Broad-leaved Laurel, Mountain Laurel
Kerria japonica	Kerria
*Koelreuteria**	Golden Rain Tree
*Laburnum anagyroides**	Common Laburnum
Laburnum X watereri	Waterer Laburnum
*Larix decidua**	European Larch
Larix decidua pendula	Weeping Larch
Larix gmelinii	Dahurian Larch
Larix laricina	American Larch, Tamarack, Hackmatack
Larix leptolepsis	Japanese Larch, Japanese Leptolepsis
Larix pendula X	Weeping Larch
Latania sp.	Fan-palm
Lespedeza bicolor	Shrub Bush-clover
Libocedrus decurrens	Incense-cedar
Ligustrum amurense	Amur Privet
Ligustrum ovalifolium	California Privet
*Liquidambar styraciflua**	Sweet Gum, Liquid Ambar
*Liriodendron tulipifera**	Tulip Tree
Lonicera canadensis	Fly Honeysuckle
Lonicera fragrantissima	Winter Honeysuckle
Lonicera gracilipes	Spangle Honeysuckle
Lonicera japonica halliana	Hall's Honeysuckle
Lonicera japonica var. *repens*	Japanese Honeysuckle Variety
Lonicera korolkowi	Blue-leaf Honeysuckle, introduced in 1880
Lonicera ledebouri	Ledebour Honeysuckle
Lonicera maacki	Amur Honeysuckle
Lonicera morrowii	Morrow Honeysuckle
Lonicera periclymenum var. *belgica*	Dutch Woodbine—"Belgian, or striped monthly (red and white)," "perhaps best known and most gen. popular."
Lonicera quinquelocularis	Mistletoe Honeysuckle
*Lonicera sempervirens**	Trumpet Honeysuckle
Lonicera spinosa alberti	Albert-thorn Honeysuckle, introduced in 1880
Lonicera syringantha	Lilac Honeysuckle, introduced in 1890
*Lonicera tartarica**	Tartarian Honeysuckle
Lonicera thibetica	Tibet Honeysuckle, introduced in 1897
Lonicera xylosteum	European Fly Honeysuckle
Lupinus arboreus var. *snow queen or albus*	Bush Lupine, Tree Lupine
Lycium barbarum	Box Thorn, Matrimony Vine
*Lyonia mariana**	Stagger Bush
Magnolia cordata	Yellow Cucumber Tree
*Magnolia denudata**	Yulan Magnolia
Magnolia kobus	Kobus Magnolia
Magnolia liliflora var. *gracilis*	Lily Magnolia
*Magnolia macrophylla**	Big Leaf Magnolia
Magnolia obovata	Whiteleaf Japanese Magnolia
*Magnolia X soulangiana**	Saucer Magnolia

Magnolia X *soulangiana* 'lennei'	Lenne's Magnolia
Magnolia soulangiana var. *norbetiana*	Saucer Magnolia cultivar
Magnolia stellata	Star Magnolia
Magnolia X *thompsoniana**	Thompson's Magnolia
*Magnolia tripetala**	Umbrella Magnolia
*Magnolia virginiana**	White Swamp Magnolia
Magnolia watsonii	Watson's Magnolia
*Mahonia aquifolium**	Oregon Holly-grape
Mahonia bealei	Leatherleaf Mahonia
Malus sp.	Dwarf Flowering Crabs—Henderson says there are seven varieties.
Malus coronaria	Garland Crab-Apple, Wild Sweet Crab
Malus floribunda	Japanese Crab Apple
Malus halliana parkmanii	Parkman Crab Apple
Malus ioensis plena	Bechtel Crab Apple, not used until after 1888
Malus sargentii	Sargent Crab Apple, not until after 1892
Malus sieboldii	Toringo Crab or Dwarf Crab
Malus spectabilis var. *riversii*	River's Crab Apple—Parsons said this was the best of double-flowering apples.
Manettia sp.	Manettia
Maurandia sp.	Maurandia
Melianthus sp.	Honey-Bush
*Menispermum canadense**	Moon-seed
Michelia fuscata	Banana Shrub
Morus alba pendula	Tea's Mulberry
Musa ensete	Banana
*Myrica cerifera**	Bayberry, Wax Myrtle
Opuntia bigelivii	Jumping Cholla, Teddy-bear Cactus
Osmanthus heterophyllus	Osmanthus
*Oxydendrum arboreum**	Sour-wood, Sorrel-tree
Pachysandra terminalis	Japanese Spurge, not used until after 1882.
Palms	Many different kinds of palms were grown both inside and out.
Pandanus veitchii	Screw-pine
*Parthenocissus quinquefolia**	Virginia Creeper
Parthenocissus tricuspidata	Boston-ivy, Japan Ivy
Parthenocissus tricuspidata var. *veitchi*	Japanese Ivy cultivar
*Paulownia tomentosa**	Empress Tree
Phellodendron amurense	Amur Cork-tree
*Philadelphus coronarius**	Sweet Mock-orange
Philadelphus coronarius var. *aureus*	Fine Dwarf Golden Variety
Philadelphus gordonianus	Mock Orange
Philadelphus grandiflorus	Big Scentless Mock-orange
Philadelphus laxus	Drooping Mock-orange
Philadelphus lemoinei var. *avalanche*	Mock Orange
Phoenix canariensis	Canary Island Date
Photinia villosa	Oriental Photinia

Physocarpus opulifolius*	Ninebark
Physocarpus opulifolius var. luteus	Ninebark Variety
Picea abies gregoryana	Gregory's Dwarf Spruce
Picea abies inversa	Weeping Norway Spruce
Picea abies virgata elata	Norway Spruce Variety
Picea engelmannii	Engelmann Spruce
Picea glauca*	American White Spruce
Picea glauca var. gloriosa	Glory of the Spruce—"warm golden tint in the midst of its young green." Parsons.
Picea orientalis*	Oriental Spruce
Picea polita	Tiger-tail Spruce
Picea pungens	Blue Spruce
Picea smithiana	Himalayan Spruce
Pieris japonica	Japanese Pieris
Pinus aristata	Bristle-cone Pine
Pinus cembra*	Swiss Stone Pine
Pinus densiflora	Japanese Red Pine
Pinus densiflora, probably var. oculus daconis	Japanese or Sun-ray Pine, Dragon's Eye Pine
Pinus lambertiana	Sugar Pine
Pinus monophylla	Single-needle Pine
Pinus mugo*	Mugho Pine, Swiss Mountain Pine
Pinus mugo var. compacta	Mughus Compacta
Pinus mugo mughus*	Dark Mughus Pine, Mugo Pine
Pinus mugo var. rostrata	"Similar to P. mugo but a tree, to 75 ft."
Pinus nepalensis	Bhotan Pine, Blue Pine, Himalyan White Pine
Pinus nigra*	Austrian Pine
Pinus nigra var. cebennensis	Cevennes Pyrenean Pine
Pinus quudrifolia	Parry Pine
Pinus strobus var. glauca dwarf form	Light Blue Dwarf White Pine
Pinus strobus nana	Dwarf White Pine
Pinus sylvestris nana	Dwarf Scotch Pine
Pinus thunbergii	Japanese Black Pine
Pinus torreyana	Torrey Pine
Platanus occidentalis*	Sycamore, Large Buttonwood
Platanus orientalis*	Oriental Plane Tree
Populus fremontii	Fremont Cottonwood
Populus nigra var. italica*	Lombardy Poplar
Populus tacamahaca, probably	Balsam Poplar
Populus tremuloides*	Quaking Aspen
Prunus sp.	Double Flowering Plums
Prunus avium 'fl. pl.	Double-flowered Mazzard Cherry, "Old White double-flowering Cherry"
Prunus cerasifera atropurpurea	Pissard Plum, used after 1885
Prunus maritima*	Beach Plum
Prunus persica fl. pl.*	Double Flowered Peach
Prunus sargentii	Sargent Cherry
Prunus spinosa fl. pl.	Sloe, Blackthorn
Prunus subhirtella pendula	Weeping Higan Cherry, Weeping Japanese Cherry
Prunus triloba	Flowering Almond

SHRUBS, TREES, AND VINES—1850–1900 (Continued)

Pseudolarix amabilis	Golden Larch
Pseudotsuga menziesii*	Douglas Fir
Pueraria thunbergiana	Kudzu-vine
Pyracantha coccinea*	Scarlet Firethorn
Quercus alba*	White Oak
Quercus borealis*	Red Oak
Quercus coccinea*	Scarlet Oak
Quercus dentata	Daimyo Oak
Quercus lyrata	Over-cup Oak
Quercus montana	Chestnut Oak
Quercus palustris	Pin Oak
Quercus phellos*	Willow Oak
Quercus robur	English Oak
Quercus robur concordia	Golden Oak, "leaves bright yellow"
Quercus robur var. *fastigiata*	Pyramidal English Oak
Quercus robur pendula	Weeping English Oak
Quercus wislizenii	Interior Live Oak
Rhododendron amoenum	Amoena Azalea
Rhododendron arborescens	Sweet Azalea
Rhododendron calendulaceum*	Flame Azalea
Rhododendron canadense*	Rhodora—"choice but not very often grown." Parsons.
Rhododendron catawbiense*	Catawba Rhododendron
Rhododendron dauricum*	Dotted-leaved Rhododendron
Rhododendron fortunei	Fortune's Rhododendron
Rhododendron X *gandavense*	Ghent Azalea
Rhododendron kaempferi	Torch Azalea, not used until after 1892
Rhododendron maximum*	Rosebay Rhododendron
Rhododendron molle	"Comparatively recent introduction"
Rhododendron mucronulatum	Korean Rhododendron
Rhododendron nudiflorum*	Pinxter Flower
Rhododendron obtusum var. *amoenum*	Flowers double, Hose-in-hose
Rhododendron occidentale	Western Azalea
Rhododendron vaseyi	Pinkshell Azalea
Rhododendron viscosum*	White Swamp Honeysuckle
Rhodotypos tetropetala	Jetbead
Rhus aromatica*	Fragrant Sumac
Rhus chinensis*	Chinese Sumac
Rhus glabra laciniata	Cut-leaved Sumach
Robinia neomexicana	New Mexican Locust
Rosa sp.	Climbing Roses: Baltimore Belle, a derivative of *R. setigera*; Queen of the Prairies, *R. setigera*
Rosa sp.	Hardy Roses: Gen. Jacqueminots; Hybrid Perpetual; Varonne Prevosts; Mad. Plantiers, a variety of *Rosa alba* X *R. gallic* and *canina* var. *dumetorum*
Rosa cathayensis var. *crimson rambler*	Crimson Rambler
Rosa eglanteria*	Sweetbrier
Rosa multiflora	Multiflora Rose

Rosa noisettiana	Noisette or Champrey Rose
Rosa odorata	Tea Rose
Rosa rugosa*	Rugosa Rose
Rosa rugosa rubra	Japan Ramanas Rose
Rosa wichuraiana	Memorial Rose, introduced in 1891
Rubus odoratus*	Flowering Raspberry
Salix alba chermesina	Redstem Willow
Salix alba var. *sericea*	Royal Willow
Salix babylonica*	Weeping Willow
Salix babylonica var. *aurea*	Golden Willow
Salix caprea	Goat Willow, Sallow Willow
Salix caprea pendula	Weeping Kilmarnock Willow
Salix pentandra	Laurel-leaved Willow
Salix repens var. *rosmarinifolia*	Rosemary-leaved Willow
Sambucus nigra aurea	European Elder
Sciadopitys verticillata	Japanese Umbrella Pine
Sciadopitys verticillata (variegated)	Variegated Japanese Umbrella Pine
Sibiraea laevigata	Sibiraea
Solanum jasminoides	Potato Vine
Sophora japonica pendula	Japan Weeping Sophora, Weeping Scholar Tree
Sorbus aucuparia*	Mountain Ash
Spiraea albiflora	Japanese White Spiraea
Spiraea bella	Spiraea
Spiraea X *billiardii*	Billiard Spiraea
Spiraea bullata	Parsons wrote in 1891, ''recently introduced from Japan.''
Spiraea X *bumalda* 'anthony waterer'	Anthony Waterer Spirea
Spiraea canescens	Hoary Spiraea
Spiraea cantoniensis	Reeve's Spirea
Spiraea chamaedrifolia	Spirea
Spiraea chamaedrifolia var. *ulmifolia*	Spirea
Spiraea douglasii	Spirea
Spiraea japonica	Japanese Spirea
Spiraea japonica atrosanguinea	Mikado Spirea
Spiraea japonica macrophylla	Japanese Spirea cultivar
Spiraea japonica ovalifolia	Mikado Spirea
Spiraea japonica, probably var. *ruberima*	Red-flowered Spirea
Spiraea X *micropetala*	*S. hypericifolia* X S. *media,* originated before 1878.
Spiraea prunifolia	Bridal Wreath
Spiraea salicifolia*	Willowleaf Spiraea
Spiraea thunbergii	Thunberg Spirea
Spiraea tomentosa*	Hardhack Spiraea, Steeplebush
Spiraea trilobata	Sometimes cultivated under name *S. blumei*
Spiraea X *vanhouttei*	Vanhoutte Spiraea
Stewartia ovata*	Mountain Stewartia
Stewartia pseudo-camellia	Japanese Stewartia, not used until after 1874
Styrax japonica	Japanese Snowbell
Symphoricarpos albus laevigatus*	Snowberry, Waxberry
Symphoricarpos orbiculatus*	Indian Currant, Coral-berry
Syringa amurensis japonica	Japanese Tree Lilac, not used until after 1876

174 SHRUBS, TREES, AND VINES—1850–1900 (Continued)

Syringa chinensis	Chinese Lilac
Syringa persica *	Persian Lilac
Syringa villosa	Late Lilac, not used until after 1882
Syringa vulgaris var. *alphonse*	Double Bluish Lilac, Lavalle Lilac
Tamarix africana	Plant usually cultivated under this name is usually *Tamarix parviflora* or Small-flowered Tamarix.
Tamarix gallica var. *indica*	French Tamarisk
Tamarix pentandra	Five-stamen Tamarisk, not used until after 1883
Taxus baccata var. *aurea*	Golden Yew
Taxus baccata var. *elegantissima*	Silver Tinted Variety
Taxus baccata var. *stricta*	Irish Yew
Taxus cuspidata	Japanese Yew
Taxus cuspidata 'nana'	Dwarf Japanese Yew
Thuja orientalis either var. *elegantissima* or *aurea*	Chinese Golden Arbor Vitae
Tilia americana *	American Linden
Tilia dasystyla	Most of what is cultivated under this name is *T. euchlora* or Crimean Linden.
Tilia, probably *platyphyllos* var. *aurea*	Golden-Barked Linden
Tilia platyphyllos var. *rubra*	Red-twigged Linden
Tilia tomentosa	White or Silver-leaved Linden
Trachelospermum jasminoides	Confederate-Jasmine
Tsuga canadensis var. 'fremd'	Canadian Hemlock cultivar
Tsuga canadensis var. *globosa*	Canadian Hemlock cultivar
Tsuga canadensis var. *macrophylla*	Canadian Hemlock cultivar
Tsuga canadensis pendula	Sargent Weeping Hemlock
Tsuga sieboldii	Southern Japanese or Siebold Hemlock
Ulmus sp.*	Elms, "majestic at all seasons"
Ulmus americana *	American Elm
Ulmus glabra camperdownii	Camperdown Elm
Ulmus parvifolia *	Chinese Elm
Ulmus pumila *	Siberian Elm
Viburnum lantana	Wayfaring Tree
Viburnum opulus	European Cranberry Bush
Viburnum opulus var. *roseum* *	Guelder Rose
Viburnum tomentosum var. *sterile* *	Japanese Snowball
Weigela florida	Rosy Weigela—"They form one of our staple plants for the construction of any gp. of shrubs." Parsons.
Weigela florida var. *variegata*	Variegated-leaved Weigelia
Weigela florida variegata (dwarf form)	Variegated Dwarf Weigelia
Weigela X *lavallei*	*W. floribunda* X *W. coraeensis*, used after 1884
Wigandia, probably *caracasana*	Wigandia
Wisteria floribunda	Japanese Wisteria
Wisteria frutescens *	American Wisteria
Wisteria sinensis var. *alba* and *purpurea* *	Chinese Wisteria
Xanthoceras sorbifolia	Chinese Flowering Chestnut, "rare and beautiful shrub"
Yucca filamentosa *	Adam's Needle, Yucca
Yucca recurvifolia	Yucca
Zelkova serrata	Graybark Elm

4

Maintaining the Restored Landscape

$\mathcal{T}$HE first question in regard to maintaining historic landscapes is whether to conduct a maintenance program according to authentic or modern practices. This is a difficult decision to make because no matter how authentic you choose to be, there are present-day factors that influence the issue.

It all boils down to a philosophy of approach which must be clearly developed before you embark on a full-fledged maintenance program. Should you give the visitor the kind of grounds and gardens he expects to see (according to his twentieth century eyes) or should you conduct your maintenance program in an educational way and show the visitor how the grounds would have looked during the period you are representing?

It is said that because visitors are accustomed to carpetlike lawns, they expect to see them when they visit a historic site. Also, many believe that visitors wish to see gardens manicured by intensive weeding, pest control, staking, and trimming. Many directors of historic sites feel that visitors will be upset if they see weeds in gravel walkways or between paving stones.

It is true that visitors will notice differences between what they may see and what they expect, but we should be educating the public concerning what landscaped grounds would have looked like during the period represented. It doesn't make sense to present a restored building, village, cemetery, or farm and then surround these historic structures with modern grounds. In fact, this has been one of the major problems with historic landscape preservation in the past. The preservation has dealt intensively with structures or complexes of structures, but the spaces between buildings have been neglected in the interpretive scheme.

If visitors are educated, either through a docent program or the printed word, they can be made to understand what the landscaped site would have been like during the represented period, and they will leave the site with a real image of its past.

Once a decision has been reached concerning whether or not to maintain the site in a period fashion, there are two other factors to consider. One is economics and the other is present-day conditions that did not exist years ago.

Economically, if you are presenting a site that is representative of the period prior to World War II, you are dealing with an era of inexpensive labor. Naturally, there were exceptions, but in general someone could be hired to weed a garden, prune shrubs, and cut the grass for just a few cents a day. Today conditions have changed and labor is costly. Therefore, we must employ modern labor-saving practices and devices without losing sight of authenticity. It is the purpose of this section to show how this can be accomplished.

There are some modern influences that were not present in the past. A good example of this is certain insect species that ravage plantings around historic structures. To let these pests destroy the site would be misrepresentation to the visitors, because the insects in question would not have been present during the period of the site. Therefore, it is wise to control the pests, using materials that are not evident and to apply these controls before the hours that visitors are allowed on the site. Another present-day intrusion to the site is the visitor himself. This problem is handled later in this section.

Lawns

Prior to the late 1860s when the lawn mower came into common use, lawns were cut with a scythe or grazed by sheep. They were cut only four or five times during the growing season, and in certain areas, such as around public buildings or battlegrounds, not that often.

178 With modern lawn-mowing equipment that is designed for weekly cutting, it is difficult to maintain a lawn that looks like one of the eighteenth or nineteenth century. Instead, what happens is that we maintain a twentieth-century lawn, which destroys the true setting for the structures.

One of the best ways to maintain a "period" lawn is *not* to use a modern lawn mower but to use a sickle-bar mower instead. This is the next best thing to scything the lawn, which would be too expensive. A grass area that is sickle-barred looks unsheared and most resembles a lawn of the period prior to lawn mowers. To achieve this effect, you should allow the lawn grasses to come almost to the seed stage and then sickle-bar them. The clippings must then be collected.

In actual practice, this system is less expensive than modern methods of lawn mowing because weekly mowing becomes unnecessary, thus saving money. In any event, regardless of your maintenance philosophy, the "scythed" effect should definitely be maintained on the grounds around forts, public buildings, eighteenth-century and early nineteenth-century cemeteries, and all sites representing a period before the 1860s.

The lawn-weed mania now prevalent among modern lawn owners did not surface until after

Fig. 108. *A landscape before the advent of lawn mowers, late 1850s. Note that the grass is long and tufted, probably mowed with a scythe about four times a year and then raked.*

World War II. It is a fact that children and servants were employed to dig weeds from select lawns, but a program to eradicate every weed in a lawn as we do now, using chemicals, should not be employed. If you want to show an authentic lawn, the common weeds of your locality should be allowed to persist.

Lawn seed is another matter to consider. Perhaps the most authentic lawn could be achieved by seeding with chaff from a haymow floor. Sophisticated mixes of lawn seed are a twentieth-century practice and not consistent with early times. In years past, when lawns were seeded, only the exceedingly wealthy purchased lawn grass seeds. As a result of seeding with haymow sweeping, eighteenth- and nineteenth-century lawns were rather coarse and rough as opposed to the carpetlike lawns of today.

The following lawn-seed mixtures (extracted from Jacob Weidenmann's *Beautifying Country Homes*, 1870) are typical of those used during the Victorian era when plain haymow chaff was considered too coarse.

Permanent Lawn Grasses in Mixture

Meadow Foxtail	1 pound
Sweet-scented Vernal Grass	1 pound
Redtop	2 pounds
Hard Fescue	3 pounds
Sheep's Fescue	1 pound
Meadow Fescue	4 pounds
Red Fescue	2 pounds
Italian Rye Grass	6 pounds
Perennial Rye Grass	8 pounds
Timothy	1 pound
June or Common Spear Grass	2 pounds
Rough-stalked Meadow Grass	2 pounds
Yellow Oat Grass	1 pound
Perennial Clover	2 pounds
Red Clover	2 pounds
White Clover	6 pounds
	44 pounds

Permanent Lawn Pastures

Meadow Foxtail	1 pound
Sweet-Scented Vernal Grass	1 pound
Orchard Grass	3 pounds
Hard Fescue	2 pounds
Sheep's Fescue	2 pounds
Meadow Fescue	2 pounds
Italian Rye Grass	6 pounds
Perennial Rye Grass	4 pounds
Timothy	7 pounds
Redtop	3 pounds
Rough-stalked Meadow Grass	3 pounds
Yellow Oat Grass	1 pound
Red Clover	2 pounds
Perennial Red Clover	2 pounds
White Clover	4 pounds
	43 pounds

For lawns to be mowed regularly, the following mixture was recommended.

Fine Lawns Frequently Mown

Crested Dogstail	10 pounds
Hard Fescue	4 pounds
Slender Leaf Sheep's Fescue	2 pounds
Perennial Rye Grass	10 pounds
Wood Meadow Grass	2 pounds
Rough-stalked Meadow Grass	1 pound
Yellow Oat Grass	1 pound
June Grass	8 pounds
White Clover	8 pounds
	46 pounds

Leaf raking on lawns in the autumn was always a standard maintenance practice. Piled leaves have always killed grass and also presented a fire hazard. Leaves were probably not raked as often during the fall season in past times but rather allowed to accumulate during the entire season or part of it. But they were then collected and composted before winter.

Perennials and Shrubs

Mulching is the continuation of a practice that is as old as gardening. Mulching means the application of a two- to three-inch layer of an organic material to the surface of soil, between plants, to keep weeds down. At the same time, it conserves soil moisture and adds organic matter to the soil. Mulches can also

180 keep a soil cool if applied when soil temperatures are still low. In recent years, plastic mulches have been used, but these are out of the question for gardens prior to 1955.

If properly applied, mulches will keep weeds to a minimum. In shrub borders or in supply nurseries, where weeds might be a severe problem, selective weed killers might be mixed with mulches to further assist in the weed-control problem. In such cases, you will want to check with the extension nursery weed-control specialist at your state land-grant university to determine which shrubs are tolerant of which weed killers, how much to apply, when to apply, and special instructions for the project in question. We feel that when maintenance costs are prohibitive, it is acceptable to employ chemicals for weed control where residue does not remain to blemish the restored landscape.

Grass clippings, compost, salt-marsh hay and weed-free straw are all authentic mulching materials. Because gardeners did not have machines to make wood chips or bark chips or any of the post-World War II mulches, it is incorrect to use them.

Mulches may be applied as soon as the soil has dried out in the spring, if you are in a temperate climate, or any time that the growing season starts and the soil temperature has risen to summertime levels.

Mulching is the answer to the weed problem in gardens and shrub borders around historic houses. Even though some weeds might be desirable, in that people in times past also had trouble keeping up with them, they must be controlled sooner or later lest the plants be obliterated by them.

Pest Control

Whether or not to spray or dust is another problem for maintainers of historic sites. Again, the visitor expectation problem begins to surface. Many feel that visitors do not wish to see buggy plants and that the plants should be sprayed to keep them free of pests.

Primitive methods of pest control were employed throughout gardening history. In the late nineteenth century, sprays such as paris green, bordeaux mixture, and nicotine products were used to eradicate certain pests. But many of the insects that attack our plants today were imported in the twentieth century. In other words, not even the pest is authentic, let alone the control. For example, Japanese beetles were introduced on nursery stock in 1916.

One way to cope with this problem is to control all of the pests introduced after the period of the restoration with modern methods. In other words, plants should be sprayed (before or after visitor hours) with the appropriate material and one that will not leave a residue. This would probably be an emulsifiable liquid, dissolved in water at the recommended rate. Dusts or wettable powders are less desirable because they will leave a residue. (Your state extension service can provide a list of materials that will control the pests in question.)

Wherever possible, try to employ old methods of pest control. Some of these methods are practical today, others are not. For example, laying large outer leaves from cabbages between plants where slugs are a problem is still an effective way to gather these pests. In the early morning the slugs will have adhered to the undersides of the cabbage leaves and the entire leaf and pest can be destroyed through burning. Another old practice is the laying of dried tobacco leaves between plants to deter certain pests. Paper collars around newly set-out annuals prevents cutworms from chewing off the seedlings at the ground level. Snuff, strong liquid manure, and charcoal dust applied close to the plants also controls cutworms.

The handpicking of insects (into water or kerosene) was one of the most common practices of insect control. Today, this is an expensive way to control insects, but if you happen to have a docent in a garden who is doing nothing else, he/she could show the old practice and it will generate much discussion about the garden.

Here are some old-time controls you may wish to experiment with.

Pest	Control
Ants	Whiskey, molasses, and water in equal parts in tumbler. Place tumbler partially in ground between plants; scoop out and kill ants after they are attracted to the concoction.
	Lay fresh bones near their hills. When bones are covered with ants, dip them in boiling water.
	Apply to young shoots strong tobacco water (water in which tobacco has steeped) to which a little starch has been added.
Aphids	Apply whale-oil soap in water to plants; also tobacco water.
	Spread among plants one ounce of flowers of sulphur mixed with a bushel of sawdust.
Bollworm on cotton	Mix four parts vinegar and one part molasses. Place in saucers on stakes among cotton plants. Moths are attracted and die.
Crow repellent	Dip pieces of cloth in sulphur and grease. Hang 10 to 12 rods apart among corn plants.
Cucumber beetles	Place onion skins in or near hills; renew periodically.
Curculio	Allow hogs to feed on fallen affected fruit in orchard. Also, apply mixture of 1 pound whale oil soap and 4 ounces flowers of sulphur in water.
Cutworms	Spread salt among plants.
Hay vermin	Spread mint leaves among the hay.
Insects affecting corn	Dust ears with flour.
Insects in general	Syringe plants with water.
	Make a strong solution with hen manure and water and apply to plants.
	Soak cotton in turpentine and place between plants.
Insects of turnips	Plant radishes among the turnips. Insects will attack radishes instead.
Mealy bugs	Apply to plants a solution of whale oil soap in water.
Onion maggots	Apply a mild brine between the plants.
Potato bugs	Powdered lime and ashes sifted on the plants.
Red spider mites	Syringe plants with water.
Rose bugs	Attract birds, especially sparrows. Pick by hand.
Rose slugs, aphids, and other rose insects	Apply every day for 10 days 1 pound whale oil soap in 8 gallons of water.
Scale	Rub off by hand with soapy water.
Squash bugs	Soak a dead fish in water for several days, then spray squash
Thrips	Tobacco smoke.

Old garden books of your region will contain many ancient pest-control practices. If you have any questions about whether or not they will work, consult your extension entomologist for advice before starting the practice. For example, some early controls, such as injecting brandy into the trunk of fruit trees to control insects, do not work.

Supporting Plants

One significant part of garden and shrub maintenance is the matter of supporting or

Fig. 109. *A practical scarecrow. C is a potato holding colored feathers. It is supported by a string (B) and suspended on a sapling (A) placed into the ground.*

staking plants that tend to fall over by their own weight. Staking is especially important if the plants are to stand erect and be seen. Also, after plants flop down and touch the ground, other plants are affected and disease problems may arise due to crowding and poor air circulation.

Certain plants require staking more than others. Tall lilies, peonies, vines in general, foxgloves, delphiniums, baptisias, or any plant that grows tall or broad or climbs should be staked. It is not enough to stake the plant after it begins to flop because it will always appear deformed in growth, having grown one-sided. Plants should be staked as they grow. After a

foot or so of growth, they should be tied to the stake which has been driven to one side of the plant or in the center of them (as in the case of broad plants such as peonies and baptisias).

Aluminum, metal, or wire stakes have become very popular since World War II, but before that time wooden stakes prevailed. In fact, if you are representing a pre-Victorian garden, you probably should use young saplings as stakes. Saplings about an inch in diameter are ideal for this purpose, and it would not be wrong to use these in a modern garden as well. From the Victorian era forward, wooden stakes that have been squared off could be used. The date when squared

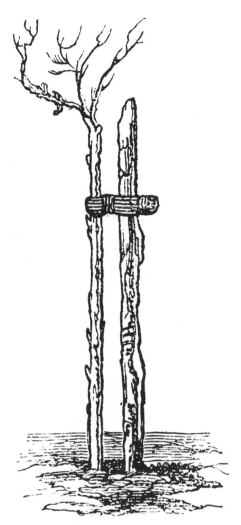

Fig. 110. *Plants were staked with sapling and twine, several strands bound together.*

young willow twigs, heavy reeds and sedges, and even raffia were used as tying material. Also, ½- to 1-inch rag strips may be used for later restorations, though these were at a premium in years past.

In place of staking, it was a common practice in the Victorian era and before to employ "pea-brushing." In fact the practice is still widely used in Europe. Depending on your situation, it may be the easiest way for you to support certain plants. Pea-brushing means to cut twigs of birch or a similar twiggy shrub long before they leaf out in the spring. These should be piled and then flattened by placing heavy weights on them. As plants begin to grow in the spring, the flattened brush is driven into the ground around the plants so that they will grow up through the brush. The brush supports the plants and the plants cover the brush. There is no need for tying or any hand work after the brush has once been installed. The trick is to install the brush early so that the plant can grow through it.

Pea-brushing works very well with broad floppy plants such as peonies, veronica, baptisia, mallows, and coreopsis. Tall slender plants such as foxgloves, lilies, and delphiniums are better staked.

Trellising is essential when vines are grown. Trellises preceding the early nineteenth century were often a simple arrangement of rectangularly crossing, 1- to 2-inch wood strips, usually a simple and forthright expression of the need to erect a support for the vine. After the Greek Revival period, trellises became a complicated and intricate arrangement of lattice work, very well integrated into the design and architecture of the house and outbuildings.

A two-volume work entitled *Gardens of Colony and State* by Alice Lockwood (Scribners, New York, 1931), though not written especially to illustrate the design of trellises, presents an excellent series of pictures of a variety of garden features actually in use.

wooden stakes became common is not a clear-cut one, so you will have to use your own judgment.

Hemp twine is a good material to use for tying plants, but it is wise to remember that where twine was not commonly available, such as in the seventeenth-, eighteenth-, and early nineteenth-century rural communities,

Fig. 111. *Trellises constructed in the rustic manner, a style that prevailed into the twentieth century.*

Pruning

Pruning is an essential part of maintaining a historic landscape. Plants are ever changing in a variety of ways, but especially in that they grow fast and can easily grow out-of-bounds. Everyday pruning is a fairly simple matter. There are many books written on the subject, and most state universities have excellent pamphlets on pruning.

The big problem is keeping old and significant plants in bounds. Large fruit trees, old roses, lilacs, fig trees, oleanders, hibiscus, camellias, or any common plant that thrives around historic sites must be controlled without destroying their contribution to the historic effect on the landscape.

When these plants are pruned back, they must look unpruned even after the operation is completed. This means that two major practices should be employed. One is renewal pruning whereby about a third of the old branches are removed each year so that new branches can replace them. The other important step is to cut these branches back to secondary branches or laterals so that no stubs remain. Visible stubs are a dead giveaway that the shrub has been severely cut back, and they also do not heal over.

While care should be taken to have the

landscape look in balance, you must also be realistic and accept the fact that pruning was employed even in ancient times. And while your main concern should be to keep your plants looking good, it is better to cut them back judiciously than to have them overrun a historic site.

Soil Fertility

Until the early nineteenth century, with but a few exceptions manures were the only fertilizer used as soil amendments. Manures are not balanced fertilizers in that they do not contain an ideal balance of the major elements (nitrogen, phosphorus, and potash). Nor do they contain many of the minor elements. For this reason, gardens used to look less lush than the well-fertilized modern gardens. Visitors should expect to see shrubs, flowers, and vegetables that are smaller and more stunted than those in most modern gardens where complete fertilizers are used.

Should your policy be to exhibit plants that grow according to modern standards, the matter of soil fertility is a simple one if you use a soil testing service (every two years) to test the soil and make specific recommendations. There is a soil testing laboratory at every state agricultural college or experiment station, and they are set up to test soil, sometimes free, but in most cases for a nominal fee. You should write to the laboratory and obtain instructions for taking a soil sample as well as other procedures before sending in the sample.

Visitor Circulation and Wear

There are several places where wear related to visitor circulation will become evident. These are within the walkway itself, at the intersection of walkways, lawn or garden areas used instead of the walkways, at the edges of and corners of flower and garden beds, and at any place where visitors congregate such as at

entrances, near rest areas, and near food concessions.

Much wear and site destruction occurs, however, because of poor or inadequate design of the circulation system. In other words, walks do not follow the general principle that the shortest distance between two points is a straight line. Nor do they take into account that people are not robots; in other words, they do not turn on sharp right angles. What we are saying is that if the circulation system is not well conceived and laid out according to the principle of the line of least resistance, you will have severe wear and tear on your site. In cases where it is impossible to redesign the circulation system because it is following an old, authentic pattern, you may have to employ strong controls to make the existing system work.

In any case, much wear can be eliminated by following a few basic principles.

1. *Lawns.* Grasses are very tough and will stand much traffic provided that the soil in which they grow does not compact excessively. When this occurs, there is not enough oxygen in the soil for optimum root growth (soil aeration), and the lawn begins to decline in quality. In such a case, the lawn must be mechanically aerated.

At best, lawns will only stand so much traffic. Where very heavy foot traffic occurs, the only solution is either to disperse the traffic through a different circulation plan or to pave the problem area.

2. *Walkways.* As mentioned previously, walkways should be laid out according to the line of least resistance. Think of people as being like water flowing along the easiest route. When resistance is encountered, wear occurs. Therefore, free-flowing walkways are desirable, and where walks intersect, the intersection should be rounded and broad, not the same width as the rest of the walkway and not at right angles.

The cheapest and oftentimes the most au-

186 thentic walkway material is gravel. However, gravel walkways are apt to grow rundown at the edges. In other words, through heavy traffic, the edge of the walk where it joins the grass wears down, thus creating a maintenance problem in that the gravel works into the grass and vice versa. Where walkways of gravel are used, an edging of wood, brick, or stone will help to confine the walk and define its edge.

Gravel walks tend to scuff and in the process gravel is carried into buildings on visitors' shoes. Especially on wood floors, this gravel acts as an abrasive, creating extensive damage. For this reason, depending on the scope of your restoration, it may pay to use a pavement such as brick, stone, flagstone, slate, or even concrete (whichever is most appropriate to the period. The initial installation will cost more than gravel, but over a period of years the maintenance may be less.

One problem with gravel, brick, and stone walks is that weeds will grow in them. Even with brick and stone, weeds grow between cracks. If traffic is unusually heavy, sometimes the weeds are worn down, but unfortunately, traffic is not that even and there are always weedy areas. Fortunately, there are some chemical weed killers that are safe to use in such situations. Again, these will vary from region to region according to type of weeds, soil conditions, weather, and a variety of factors. For this reason, write to your extension agronomist or weed control specialist at your state land-grant college. Many of these weed killers not only destroy the weeds on contact but will last throughout the entire season making weed control a "one shot" operation.

Historically, weeds would have been left in most public areas or around nongarden landscapes. But in the gardens of the wealthy who employed many servants, most of them would have been removed.

Gravel walks were very common in the seventeenth, eighteenth, and early nineteenth century. Here is a description for laying a gravel walk taken from Mackenzie's *Five Thousand Recipes in the Useful and Domestic Arts* published in 1831:

The bottom should be laid with lime rubbish, large flint stones, or other hard matter, for eight to ten inches thick, to keep the weeds from growing through, and over this the gravel is to be laid six or eight inches thick. This should be laid rounding up in the middle, by which means the larger stones will run off to the sides and may be raked away; for the gravel should never be screened before it is laid on. It is a common mistake to lay these walks too round, which not only makes them uneasy to walk upon, but takes off from their apparent breadth. One inch in five feet is sufficient proportion for the rise in the middle; so that a walk of twenty feet wide should be four inches higher at the middle than at the edges, and so in proportion. As soon as the gravel is laid it should be raked, and the large stones thrown back again; then the whole should be rolled both lengthwise and crosswise; and the person who draws the roller should wear shoes with flat heels, that he may make no holes, because holes made in a new walk are not easily remedied. The walks should always be rolled three or four times after very hard showers, from which they will bind more firmly than otherwise they could ever be made to do.

3. *Edges of gardens.* Sometimes where traffic is unusually heavy and where walkways are not wide enough, visitors will cut across the corners of gardens, thus destroying the plants. This is a worldwide problem.

The British have devised an excellent type of looped rod, the thickness of a concrete reinforcing rod. These rods are bent to form a half circle and the two ends are driven into the ground. Several of these are used in succession to make a little fence where traffic cross-cutting is a problem. Wood saplings may be used in the same way. Willow, hickory, or any supple wood is best. Wooden loops have the advantage of appearing "more authentic" in

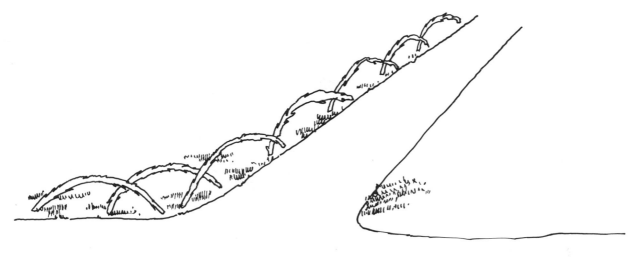

Fig. 112. *Arches made of iron or tree boughs and set into the ground to control pedestrian traffic. Each arch is about 18 to 24 inches high.*

certain restorations. Therefore, they may be more desirable. However, they have the obvious disadvantage of rotting out at the base and having to be changed on a yearly basis.

A heavier post-type barrier may also be used to ward off cross traffic. This is merely a 4- to 6-inch diameter log pegged across two posts set into the ground. While these are effective, their scale might be too heavy in a garden situation and they also may appear too rustic. You must decide which system you will use.

4. *Controls.* Where cross traffic is a problem and the walkways cannot be designed to eliminate it, strong controls must be used. This means that fences, walls, hedges, or some other impenetrable barrier must be installed to physically divert traffic. Control systems selected must be of proper scale with the space in which they are used and also of compatible materials. Often hedges are used because they blend easily with any setting. If hedges are

used, it is important to plant them thickly so that people will not walk through them. Until they fill in, a cheap fence may be installed along with the hedge and removed as soon as the hedge grows solid. There are many hedge materials that are attractive in flower, foliage color, and texture. In addition, many of these have thorns which make them very effective barriers. Your local extension service can provide a list of such material appropriate to your region.

Vandalism and Site Security

Naturally, some vandalism occurs because there are vandals afoot who practice destruction. But in many cases, vandalism is committed because of aggravation experienced by an individual. In other words, something happens to make that person aggressive. This might be too many signs that say "do this" or

Fig. 113. *Rustic control barriers can be built of logs such as those shown here in this period sketch.*

especially "DON'T do this"; a circulation system that doesn't work; inadequate restroom facilities; no place to sit and rest; confusion generated by a plan that doesn't read properly to the visitor; and many other factors.

It is important to generate a good psychological image. Here are some suggestions.

1. The circulation and layout should be well thought out and work with a minimum of confusion and irritation.

2. The system should be so well designed that no "do" and "don't" signs are needed. When signs must be used, simple, vandal-proof signs are a must. In other words, the sign should consist of a simple board with no moulding or trim, if possible. It should be of a material that does not easily break or bend such as heavy metal or plywood. The signs should be carefully and securely affixed to their supports, preferably a structure rather than a freestanding post.

3. Inviting entrances and pleasant exits go a long way in creating a friendly image and one that tends to reduce vandalism. Entrances are made inviting by being large enough to absorb an average crowd, having an effective and efficient admitting procedure, being well landscaped, having no worn or untidy areas, having places for people to sit and wait for other members of their party, and immediately

Fig. 114. *Grass will not grow in compacted soil. This low, temporary fence is changed every few days, from one side to the other, so that compaction will not kill the grass. Foot traffic passes over the slatted board matt.*

orienting the visitor so that confusion is eliminated.

Pleasant exits should also be well land-scaped. In addition, there should be benches where people can wait, clear routing to rest facilities, tidy and well-kept walkways to the exit vehicle, and places for people to picnic.

4. Another part of creating a good image is good housekeeping. The moment deterioration of any type is visible, it invites more of the same, usually in the form of vandalism. For this reason, litter receptacles are important at strategic spots on the site. Such places would be near rest areas, at major circulation nodes, near parking areas, near entrances and exits,

near concessions, and where litter problems have been observed to exist.

Oftentimes on preservation sites an attempt is made to make litter receptacles appear in period. For example, tiny iron kettles are placed around or hollow tree trunks standing on end are used. These are too contrived and do not read as intended. While care should be taken to select a litter receptacle that is in scale and harmony with the site, it should be a forthright expression of the problem and read as such. After all, there were no litter receptacles in the 1700s so why should we use a "period piece"?

5. Another maintenance problem is site se-

190 curity. Again, much can be accomplished along these lines by creating a friendly "we-care-for-you" image. Also, tip-top maintenance encourages pride in a site. However, we are all aware that this is not the whole answer.

Site security is handled in a variety of ways, each of them effective in particular respects. One such way is to fence the site heavily by using a tall, impenetrable fence, but one that can be seen through. The most effective fence for such purposes is a metal picket-type fence, six to eight feet tall, with pointed rod pickets. Another good solution is a solid wood fence with a strand of barbed wire nailed to the top moulding. But such a fence invites graffiti on its exterior side and seems exclusionary in that one cannot see through it. Hence, it may invite vandalism. Steel mesh fences are effective but unattractive and they also give an unfriendly image. This type of fence is associated with prisons or other institutions that exclude or confine. Remember that in selecting a fence, it should be strong enough to do the job yet be in harmony with the site and still create a friendly image. See-through fences are better in this regard than solid ones.

One concept of site security is why fence at all? Many sites have found that by having free circulation through the site, less vandalism occurs. This means that if admission is charged, the visitors must be checked at each building to see that their fee has been paid. This concept may not work in every case, but in some cases where there is a complex of buildings and a watchman, it will be effective. It also works extremely well where a resident curator is on the site or where portions of the site are inhabited.

Appendix

Worcester County Horticultural Society

30 Elm Street, Worcester, Mass. 01608

Descriptions of Old Apple Varieties in Preservation Orchard (At Old Sturbridge Village, Sturbridge, Mass.)

ALEXANDER: Origin, Russia before 1817. Season, September and October to November. Color, red or striped. Flavor, mild subacid, fair to good. Uses, more suitable for cooking than dessert.

AMERICAN BEAUTY-STERLING: Origin, Sterling, Mass. Season, December to April. Color, very dark. Flavor, subacid, aromatic, very good quality. Uses, dessert.

BALDWIN-WOODPECKER: Origin, Wilmington, near Lowell, Mass., about 1740. Season, November to March. Color, bright red. Flavor, agreeable subacid, somewhat aromatic. Uses, well adapted for cooking and dessert.

BEN DAVIS: Origin, possibly Tennessee, Kentucky, or Virginia, early in 1800. Season, January to June. Color, bright deep red or red-striped. Flavor, mildly subacid, somewhat aromatic. Uses, not too acceptable for home use.

BENONI: Origin, Dedham, Mass., about 1832. Season, August to September. Color, orange-yellow with red, striped with carmine. Flavor, pleasant subacid. Uses, dessert.

BLACK GILLIFLOWER-SHEEPNOSE: Origin, possibly Connecticut, early 1800. Season, October to January. Color, red to dark purple. Flavor, rich, mild subacid. Uses, good for dessert.

BLUE PEARMAIN: Origin, supposed to be an American variety, about 1800. Season, October to January. Color, red with blue bloom. Flavor, mild aromatic. Uses, home and local market.

CHENANGO: Origin, Lebanon, N.Y., or Connecticut, about 1850. Season, August through September. Color, yellowish white striped with red. Flavor, mild subacid, very aromatic. Uses, good for cooking and dessert.

COX ORANGE: Origin, England, about 1830. Season, September to January. Color, red and yellow. Flavor, rich, decidedly aromatic. Uses, good for home use.

DUCHESS OF OLDENBURG: Origin, Russia, early 1800. Season, late August and September. Color, stripes of red shaded with crimson. Flavor, sprightly subacid, aromatic. Uses, cooking; too much acid for dessert.

EARLY HARVEST: Origin, unknown, before 1800. Season, July and August. Color, pale yellow. Flavor, briskly subacid, but becoming milder. Uses, excellent for dessert or cooking.

ENGLISH BEAUTY-DOMINE: Origin uncertain, possibly Maryland. A striped apple of the Rambo class. Good keeper. Season, November to March. Very firm, tender, juicy, mild subacid, aromatic flavor.

ESOPUS SPITZENBURG: Origin, Esopus, Ulster County, New York, early 1800 or before. Season, November to February. Color, bright red with yellow dots. Flavor, very good, subacid. Uses, choice dessert fruit; also good cooking.

FALLAWATER: Origin, Pennsylvania, early 1800. Season, November to March. Color, yellow, blushed with deep pinkish red. Flavor, mildly sweet. Uses, desirable for cooking.

FALL PIPPIN: Origin, unknown. Season, late September to January. Color, yellow. Flavor, agreeably subacid, aromatic. Uses, very good cooking, good dessert.

FAMEUSE-SNOW: Origin, possibly France, one of the oldest varieties. Season, October to mid-winter. Color, light, bright red deepening to purple, with somewhat striped appearance. Flavor, sweetish, aromatic. Uses, very good for dessert.

192 GOLDEN RUSSET: Origin, unknown. Season, December to April. Color, golden with bronze cheeks. Flavor, agreeably subacid, aromatic. Uses, excellent for dessert and cooking.

GRAVENSTEIN: Origin, possibly Germany. Season, late September to early November. Color, orange-yellow with stripes of red. Flavor, sprightly subacid, aromatic. Uses, excellent for cooking.

GRIMES GOLDEN: Origin, West Virginia, before 1800. Season, November to January. Color, rich golden yellow. Flavor, rich, aromatic. Uses, excellent cooking or dessert.

HIGH TOP SWEET: An old variety of obscure origin, but a great favorite in the early days of the Plymouth Colony. A small, yellow, very sweet apple ripening in August.

HUBBARDSTON: Origin, Hubbardston, Mass., early 1800. Season, October to January. Color, yellow or greenish mottled with red. Flavor, sprightly, becoming mild subacid, mingled with sweet. Uses, excellent for dessert.

JONATHAN: Origin, Woodstock, N.Y., early 1800. Season, November to January. Color, brilliant red. Flavor, very aromatic, sprightly subacid. Uses, good dessert or cooking.

LADY: Origin, France, 1600 or before. Season, December to May. Color, beautiful red and yellow. Flavor, subacid, becoming nearly sweet. Uses, decoration and dessert.

MAIDEN'S BLUSH: Origin, unknown, early 1800. Season, September to November. Color, pale lemon yellow with crimson cheeks. Flavor, subacid. Uses, good cooking.

McINTOSH: Origin, Ontario, about 1820. Season, October to December. Color, bright deep red. Flavor, aromatic, perfumed, subacid, becoming nearly sweet. Uses, very good dessert.

MOTHER: Origin, Bolton, Mass., early 1800. Season, September to January. Color, golden yellow nearly covered with bright deep red. Flavor, very mild subacid, aromatic. Uses, dessert.

NODHEAD-JEWETT: Origin, Hollis, N.J. Season, October to February. Color, dark red with blue bloom. Flavor, mild, subacid or nearly sweet, aromatic. Uses, dessert fruit.

NORTHERN SPY: Origin, East Bloomfield, N.J., about 1800. Season, November to February. Color, bright red with delicate bloom. Flavor, sprightly aromatic, subacid. Uses, cooking or dessert.

OPALESCENT: Introduced about 1899, Xenia, Ohio. Season, November to February. Color, bright pale yellow overspread with dark deep red, glossy. Flavor, mild subacid, aromatic, good to very good. Fruit, large.

PALMER GREENING-WASHINGTON ROYAL: Origin, Sterling, Mass. Season, October and November. Color, yellow or greenish, shaded with red. Flavor, mild eventually becoming sweet. Uses, dessert.

PECK'S PLEASANT: Belongs to the same group as Rhode Island Greening. It probably also originated in Rhode Island. A high-quality dessert apple, yellow with orange-red blush. Season, October to March.

PORTER: Origin, Sherburne, Mass., about 1800. Season, September to November. Color, yellow marked with red. Flavor, agreeably aromatic. Uses, cooking and dessert.

PRIMATE: Origin, Onondaga County, N.Y., about 1840. Season, August and September. Color, pale yellow or whitish, slightly blushed. Flavor, subacid, aromatic. Uses, dessert.

PUMPKIN SWEET-POUND SWEET: Origin, Manchester, Conn. Season, October to January. Color, light and dark green with whitish scarf skin. Flavor, decidedly sweet with peculiar flavor. Uses, baking and canning.

RAMSDELL SWEET: Origin, Thompson, Conn. Season, October to February. Color, dark red prevailing. Flavor, very sweet. Uses, dessert.

RED ASTRACHAN: Origin, Russia. Season, late July to September. Color, yellow with dark red splashes. Flavor, brisk subacid, aromatic, slightly astringent. Uses, early for cooking, later for dessert.

RED JUNE: Origin, North Carolina. Season, July to early winter. Color, deep red over yellow. Flavor, brisk, subacid. Uses, dessert.

RIBSTON: Origin, Yorkshire, England, about 1700. Season, late September to December. Color, yellow or greenish with dull red. Flavor, pleasantly subacid, rich. Uses, cooking and dessert.

RHODE ISLAND GREENING: Origin, near Newport, R.I., about 1700. Season, October to March. Color, green, later yellow. Flavor, sprightly subacid, peculiarly flavored. Uses, very good cooking and dessert.

ROXBURY RUSSET: Origin, Roxbury, Mass., about 1649. Season, December to May. Color, greenish to yellowish-brown russet. Flavor, sprightly subacid. Uses, good to very good for home use.

RUSSET PEARMAIN-HUNT RUSSET: Originated on Hunt Farm, Concord, Mass. Season, January to April. A good keeper of high quality, golden russet with bright red cheek.

SMOKEHOUSE: Origin, Lancaster County, Pa., early 1800. Season, October to February. Color, neither distinctly yellow nor red. Flavor, delicately aromatic, agreeable flavor. Uses, dessert.

SOPS OF WINE: Origin, England, very ancient variety. Season, August to October. Color, dark crimson red. Flavor, subacid, aromatic. Uses, dessert apple.

SUTTON: Origin, Sutton, Mass., before 1848. Season, November to March. Color, lively yellow striped with bright red. Flavor, mild subacid. Uses, dessert.

SWEET BOUGH-AUGUST SWEET: Origin, American, early 1800. Season, July to September. Color, greenish-yellow to yellowish white. Flavor, sweet. Uses, cooking and eating.

SWEET WINESAP: Origin, Pa., before 1869. son, November to April. Color, pale yellow overspread with red. Flavor, distinctly sweet. Uses, cooking and dessert.

TOLMAN SWEET: Origin, Dorchester, Mass. Season, November to January. Color, yellow with dots. Flavor, decidedly sweet. Uses, cooking.

THOMPKINS KING: Origin, Warren County, N. J., before 1804. Season, October to December. Color,

beautiful red with contrasting yellow. Flavor, aromatic subacid. Uses, dessert or cooking.

TWENTY OUNCE: Origin, possibly Connecticut. Season, late September to early winter. Color, green becoming yellow with broad stripes of red. Coarse, subacid. Uses, cooking good, dessert fair.

WAGENER: Origin, Penn Yan, N.Y., about 1800. Season, October to February. Color, bright red contrasting yellow. Flavor, subacid, aromatic. Uses, cooking or dessert.

WASHINGTON STRAWBERRY: Origin, Washington County, N.Y. Season, September to early winter. Color, waxy greenish or yellow mottled with red. Flavor, pleasant subacid, sprightly. Uses, cooking and dessert.

WEALTHY: Origin, Excelsior, Minn. Season, October to early or mid-winter. Color, bright red. Flavor, agreeably subacid, somewhat aromatic. Uses, cooking or dessert, very hardy.

WELLINGTON BLOOMLESS-DUMELOW: Origin, England, early 1800. Season, November to March or April. Color, yellow. Flavor, brisk, subacid, slightly aromatic. Uses, cooking; too much acid for dessert.

WESTFIELD-SEEK-NO-FURTHER: Origin, Westfield, Mass. Season, late fall and early winter. Color, creamy yellow striped with dull red. Flavor, rich, sometimes astringent, peculiarly aromatic. Uses, dessert, an old favorite.

WHITE PIPPIN: Origin, unknown. Season, November to May. Color, yellow. Flavor, coarse, sprightly subacid. Uses, cooking or dessert, valuable variety.

WILLIAMS-LADY APPLE: Origin, Roxbury, Mass., about 1760. Season, late August and early September. Color, bright red overlaying yellow. Flavor, mild subacid, aromatic. Uses, dessert.

WOLF RIVER: Origin, Wisconsin. Season, September to December. Color, pale bright yellow or greenish, mottled with bright deep red. Flavor, subacid, a little aromatic. Very large.

YELLOW BELLFLOWER: Origin, New Jersey. Season, December to February. Color, pale lemon-yellow. Flavor, aromatic, acid. Uses, good for cooking early in season, later when acidity is subdued; good for eating, large fruit.

YELLOW NEWTOWN-ALBERMARLE: Origin, Newton, Long Island, N.Y. Season, February to May. Color, bright yellow with pinkish blush. Flavor, highly aromatic. Uses, cooking and dessert, one of the best.

YELLOW TRANSPARENT: Origin, Russia. Season, July to September. Color, clear yellow. Flavor, sprightly subacid, pleasant but not highly flavored. Uses, excellent for cooking, acceptable for dessert. One of the best early apples.

A Useful Bibliography

Abercrombie, John. *The Complete Wall-tree Pruner.* London, 1783.

Abercrombie, John. *The Gardener's Daily Assistant.* London, 1786.

"American Garden Milestones." *Flower Grower Magazine,* vol. 46, no. 12 (December 1959), p. 24.

American Historical Catalogue Collection. *Ornamental Iron Work.* Janes, Kirtland and Company, 1870. Princeton, N.J.:Pyne Press, 1971.

The American Rose Culturist. New York, 1852.

Anthony, John. *Discovering Period Gardens.* Shire Publications, Ltd., 1972.

Authentic Plant Materials for Gardens of Colonial Williamsburg. Williamsburg Garden Symposium Mimeograph. Williamsburg, Va., 1968.

Bailey, Liberty Hyde. *The Standard Cyclopedia of American Horticulture.* 3 vols. New York: The Macmillan Company, 1933.

Bailey, Liberty Hyde, and Bailey, Ethel Zoe. (Revised and expanded by staff of Bailey Hortorium.) *Hortus Third.* New York: The Macmillan Company, 1976.

Bartram, John. *Diary of a Journey through the Carolinas, Georgia, and Florida, 1765–66.* Philadelphia: American Philosophical Society, 1942.

Bartram, William. *Travels through North and South Carolina, Georgia, East and West Florida.* 1791.

Betts, Edwin Morris. *Thomas Jefferson's Garden Book.* Memoirs, vol. 22. Philadelphia: The American Philosophical Society, 1944.

Bigelow, Jacob. *Florula Bostoniensis.* Boston, 1824 and 1840.

Bourne, H. The Florist's Manual. Boston: Monroe and Francis, Publishers, 1833.

Bridgeman, Thomas. *The American Gardener's Assistant.* Philadelphia, 1832.

Bridgeman, Thomas. *The Kitchen Gardener's Assistant.* New York, 1836.

Bridgeman, Thomas. *The Young Gardener's Assistant.* New York, 1837 and 1847.

Brooklyn Botanical Gardens. *Origins of American Horticulture.* Plants and Gardens, vol. 23, no. 3, Autumn, 1967.

Buist, Robert. *The American Flower Garden Directory.* Philadelphia, 1841.

Buist, Robert. *The Family Kitchen Gardener.* New York, 1847.

Clapham, A. R.; Tuton, T. G.; and Warburg, E. F. *Flora of the British Isles.* Cambridge: Cambridge University Press, 1952.

Clifford, Derek. *A History of Garden Design.* New York: Frederick A. Praeger, 1963.

Cobbett, William. *The American Gardener.* London, 1821.

The Compleat Planter and Cyderist. London, 1685.

Conover, Herbert S. *Grounds Maintenance Handbook.* 3d. ed. New York: McGraw-Hill Book Company, 1977.

Department of Housing and Urban Development. *Preserving Historic America.* Washington, D.C.: Government Printing Office, 1966.

Downing, Andrew Jackson. *Landscape Gardening and Rural Architecture.* New York: G. P. Putnam and Company, 1853.

Downing, Andrew Jackson. *Rural Essays.* New York, 1853.

Dudley, Mrs. A. T. *The Moffatt-Ladd House and Its Garden.*

Eaton, Amos. *Manual of Botany.* 3d. ed. Albany, 1822.

Elliott, F. R. *Handbook of Practical Landscape Gardening.* Rochester, N.Y.: D. M. Dewey, Publisher, 1885.

Ely, Helena Rutherford. *Another Hardy Garden Book.* New York: The Macmillan Company, 1912.

Ely, Helena Rutherford. *A Woman's Hardy Garden.* New York: Grossett & Dunlap Publishers, 1903.

Evelyn, John. *Sylva.* London, 1670.

Faris, John T. *Old Gardens in and about Philadelphia.* Indianapolis: The Bobbs-Merrill Company, 1932.

Favretti, Rudy J. *Early New England Gardens, 1620–1840.* Old Sturbridge Village, Sturbridge, Mass., 1962.

Favretti, R. J., and Favretti, Joy P. *For Every House a Garden.* Chester, Conn.: Pequot Press, 1977.

Fein, Albert. *Frederick Law Olmsted and the American Environmental Tradition.* New York: George Braziller, 1972.

Fessenden, Thomas Green. *The American Kitchen Gardener.* New York, 1852.

Fessenden, Thomas Green. *The New American Gardener.* Boston, 1830.

Fisher, Robert B. *The Mount Vernon Gardens.* The

Bibliography

196

Mount Vernon Ladies' Association, Mount Vernon, Va., 1960.

Fogg, John M. "Common Weeds from Europe." In *Origins of American Horticulture, A Handbook.* vol. 23, no. 3. New York: Brooklyn Botanic Garden, 1967.

Gerard, John. *The Herball, or General Historie of Plantes.* London, 1636.

Gillon, Edmond V., Jr., and Lancaster, Clay. *Victorian Houses.* New York: Dover Publishers, 1973.

Gleanings from the Most Celebrated Books on Husbandry, Gardening, and Rural Affairs. Philadelphia, 1803.

Gothein, Marie Louise. *The History of Garden Art.* New York: E. P. Dutton and Company, 1928.

Hedrick, V. P. *A History of Horticulture in America to 1860.* New York: Oxford University Press, 1950.

Hedrick, V. P., et al. *The Cherries of New York.* Annual Report, New York Agricultural Experiment Station. No. 22, vol. 2, pt. II. J. B. Lyon Company, Albany, N.Y., 1915.

Hedrick, V. P., et al. *The Grapes of New York.* Annual Report, New York Agricultural Experiment Station. No. 24, vol. 2, pt. II. J. B. Lyon Company, Albany, N.Y., 1917.

Hedrick, V. P., et al. *The Peaches of New York.* Annual Report, New York Agricultural Experiment Station. No. 24, vol. 2, pt. II. J. B. Lyon Company, Albany, N.Y., 1917.

Hedrick, V. P., et al. *The Pears of New York.* Annual Report, New York Agricultural Experiment Station. No. 29, vol. 2, pt. II. J. B. Lyon Company, Albany, N.Y., 1921.

Hedrick, V. P., et al. *The Plums of New York.* Annual Report, New York Agricultural Experiment Station. No. 28, vol. 3, pt. II. J. B. Lyon Company, Albany, N.Y., 1911.

Hedrick, V. P., et al. *The Small Fruit of New York.* Annual Report, New York Agricultural Experiment Station. No. 31, pt. II. J. B. Lyon Company, Albany, N.Y., 1925.

Hedrick, V. P., ed. *Sturtevant's Notes on Edible Plants.* Annual Report, New York Agricultural Experiment Station. No. 27, vol. 2, pt. II. J. B. Lyon Company, Albany, N.Y., 1919.

Henderson, Charles. *Henderson's Picturesque Gardens.* New York: Peter Henderson, Company, 1901.

Hill, John. *Eden: Or a Compleat Book of Gardening.* London, 1757.

Hill, John. *The Family Herbal.* Bungay, 1812.

Hollingsworth, Buckner. *Her Garden Is Her Delight.* New York: The Macmillan Company, 1962.

Hughes, William. *The Flower Garden and Compleat Vinyard.* 3d. ed. London, 1683.

Hunt, John D., and Willis, Peter. *The Genius of the Place.* New York: Harper & Row, 1975.

James River Garden Club. *Historic Gardens of Virginia.* Richmond, 1923.

Johnson, F. B., and Waterman, T. T. *Early Architecture of North Carolina.* Chapel Hill, N. C.: University of North Carolina Press, 1941 and 1947.

Johnson, Louisa. *Every Lady Her Own Flower Gardener.* Charleston, 1842.

Josselyn, John. *New England Rarities.* London, 1673.

Kalm, Peter. *Travels in North America, The America of 1750.* 2 vols. New York: Dover Publications, 1964.

Kemp, Edward. *How to Lay Out a Garden.* New York: John Wiley and Son, 1889.

Kern, G. M. *Practical Landscape Gardening.* Cincinnati, Ohio: Moore, Wilstach, Keyes and Company, 1855.

King, Mrs. Francis. *Chronicles of the Garden.* New York: Chas. Scribner's Sons, 1925.

King, Mrs. Francis. *The Well Considered Garden.* New York: Chas. Scribner's Sons, 1916.

Laurence, John. *The Fruit Garden Kalender.* London, 1718.

Lawson, William. *The Country Housewife's Garden.* London, 1617.

Leighton, Ann. *American Gardens in the Eighteenth Century.* Boston: Houghton Mifflin Company, 1976.

Leighton, Ann. *Early American Gardens.* Boston: Houghton Mifflin Company, 1970.

Lockwood, Alice B. *Gardens of Colony and State.* 2 vols. New York: Chas. Scribner and Sons, 1931.

Loudon, John Claudius. *An Encyclopaedia of Gardening.* London, 1827.

Lowery. *Spanish Settlements in the United States, Florida from 1513 to 1561.* New York: Putnam, 1905.

Lowery. *Spanish Setlements in the United States, Florida from 1562 to 1574.* New York: Putnam, 1905.

McMahon, Bernard. *The American Gardener's Calendar*. 8th ed. Philadelphia, 1832.

Manks, Dorothy S. "Early American Nurserymen and Seedsmen." In *Origins of American Horticulture, A Handbook*. Vol. 23, no. 3. New York: Brooklyn Botanic Garden, 1967.

Manks, Dorothy S. "How the American Nursery Trade Began." In *Origins of American Horticulture, A Handbook*. Vol. 23, no. 3. New York: Brooklyn Botanic Garden, 1967.

Mason, George. *An Essay on Design in Gardening*. London, 1768.

Massingham, Betty. *Miss Jekyll*. London: Country Life Ltd., 1966.

Mawe, Thomas. *Every Man His own Gardener*. London, 1776.

Miller Phillip. *The Gardener's and Botanist's Dictionary*. London, 1807.

Miller, Phillip. *The Gardeners Kalendar*. London, 1765.

Noel Hume, Audrey. *Archaeology and the Colonial Gardener*. Colonial Williamsburg Archaelogical series no. 7. Williamsburg, Va.: Colonial Williamsburg Foundation, 1974.

Nuttall, Thomas. *The Genera of North American Plants*. Philadelphia, 1818.

Orcutt, Phillip Dana. *The Moffatt-Ladd House—Its Garden and Its Period*.

Perkins, H. C. et al. *The Practical Florist*. Newburyport, 1833.

Powell, Summer Chicton. *Puritan Village*. Middletown, Conn.: Wesleyan University Press, 1963.

Reps, John W. *The Making of Urban America*. Princeton, N.J.: Princeton University Press, 1965.

Richardson, Josiah. *The New England Farrier and Family Physician*. Exeter, N.H., 1828.

Robinson, William. *The English Flower Garden*. London: John Murray, 1901.

Sayers, Edward. *The American Flower Garden Companion*. New York, 1838.

Shaffer, E. T. H. *Carolina Gardens*. Chapel Hill, N.C.: University of North Carolina Press, 1939.

Slade, Daniel D. *Evolution of Horticulture in New England*. New York: Knickerbocker Press, 1895.

Squibb, Robert. *The Gardener's Kalendar for South Carolina and North Carolina*. Printed for A. Timothy. Charlestown, S.C., 1842.

Stuart, Henry. *The Planter's Guide*. 1st. American ed. New York, 1832.

Tabor, Grace. *Old Fashioned Gardening*. New York: Robert McBryde Company, 1925.

Taylor, Raymond L. *Plants of Colonial Days*. Williamsburg, Va.: Colonial Williamsburg, 1968.

Thorburn, Grant. *The Gentleman and Gardener's Kalendar*. 3d. ed. New York, 1821.

Waite, Diana S., ed. *Architectural Elements*. American Historical Catalogue Collection. Princeton, N.J.: Pyne Press, 1972.

Watts, May T. *Reading the Landscape*. New York: The Macmillan Company, 1957.

Wells, B. W. *Natural Gardens of North Carolina*. Auspices of the Garden Club of North Carolina. Chapel Hill, N.C.: University of North Carolina Press, 1932.

Wheatley, William. *Observations on Modern Gardening*. London, 1770.

Whiffen, Marcus. *American Architecture Since 1780: A Guide to the Styles*. Cambridge, Mass.: M.I.T. Press, 1969.

Wilder, Marshall P. *The Horticulture of Boston and Vicinity*. Boston: Tolman and White, 1881.

Worcester County Horticultural Society. *List and Order Sheet of Scions for Grafting*. Worcester County Horticultural Society, 30 Elm Street, Worcester, Mass.

Wright, Richardson. *The Story of Gardening*. New York: Dodd, Mead & Company, 1934.

Wyman, Donald. "Introductory Dates of Familiar Trees, Shrubs and Vines." In *Origins of American Horticulture, A Handbook*. Vol. 23, no. 3. New York: Brooklyn Botanic Garden, 1967.

Acknowledgments

The illustrations in this book were assembled from many sources. For their great help and for use of the illustrations identified below by number, authors and publisher make grateful acknowledgment to those sources.

Fig. 1, from *The Gardiner's Labyrinth*, by Thomas Hill, 1577.

Fig. 2, 17, from *Picturesque America*, edited by William Cullen Bryant, vol. I, 1874.

Fig. 3, 73, 74, 104, 108, 113, from *Gleason's Pictorial* (clipped, no date). Loaned by Mrs. Florence Waxman.

Fig. 4, 8, 9, 81, 89, 90, 91, 92, 93, 94, 112, drawn by John Alexopoulos, plan by R. J. Favretti.

Fig. 5, through the courtesy of Old Sturbridge Village, Sturbridge, Mass. (Oil on canvas, 20" × 24", by Samuel Gerry, 1849.)

Fig. 6, 7, loaned by Mrs. Joseph Grills, Ledyard, Conn.

Fig. 19, 20, 21, 49, 50, 51, 82, 88, 114, photographs by the authors.

Fig. 10, *Historical Collections of the State of New York*, by John Warner Barber, 1851.

Fig. 11, 71, *Historical Collections of Every Town in Connecticut*, by John Warner Barber, 1836.

Fig. 12, *Gleason's Pictorial*, vol. IV, no. 13, March 26, 1853. Loaned by Mrs. Florence Waxman.

Fig. 13, 14, 35, lithograph of Sarony, Major, and Knapp for *D. T. Valentine's Manual*, 1861. Loaned by Mrs. Florence Waxman.

Fig. 15, 18, courtesy of the Colonial Williamsburg Foundation, Williamsburg, Va.

Fig. 16, plan for the garden at the Mission House, Stockbridge, Mass. From a drawing by Mrs. Loring Conant, 1962.

Fig. 22, courtesy of the Mt. Vernon Ladies Assn., Mt. Vernon, Va.

Fig. 23, courtesy of the Thomas Jefferson Memorial Foundation, Monticello, Charlottesville, Va.

Fig. 24, courtesy of the Society for the Preservation of New England Antiquities, Boston, Mass.

Fig. 25, courtesy of the Litchfield Historical Society, Litchfield, Conn. View of Sharon, by Ralph Earl.

Fig. 26, courtesy of the Litchfield Historical Society. Mrs. Judson Canfield, by Ralph Earl, oil on canvas, 46" × 47", 1796.

Fig. 27, courtesy of the Essex Institute, Salem, Mass.

Fig. 28, 46, 55, from *Landscape Gardening and Rural Architecture*, by A. J. Downing, 1849.

Fig. 29, from *Kemp on Landscape Gardening*, by Edward Kemp, 1889.

Fig. 30, lithograph by Geo. Hayward for *D. T. Valentine's Manual*, 1858. Loaned by Mrs. Florence Waxman.

Fig. 31, courtesy of the Ladies Hermitage Assn., Nashville, Tenn.

Fig. 32, 40, from *Beautifying Country Homes* by Jacob Weidenmann, 1870.

Fig. 33, 36, 39, from *The Horticulturist* (new series) vol. III, 1853 (frontispiece).

Fig. 34, courtesy of Rosedown, St. Francisville, La.

Fig. 37, 38, from *The Horticulturist* (new series) vol. III, 1857.

Fig. 41, 99, 105, from *Vick's Illustrated Monthly*, vol. I, 1878, Rochester, N.Y.

Fig. 42, 43, 67, 69, 106, 107, from *Picturesque Gardens*, by Charles Henderson, 1901.

Fig. 44, stereoscope view, published by J. F. Jarvis, Washington, D.C.

Fig. 45, courtesy of the Antiquarian and Landmarks Soc., Hartford, Conn.

Fig. 47, by A. C. Warren, printed by D. Appleton and Co., N.Y., 1873. Loaned by Mrs. Florence Waxman.

Fig. 48, 52, 57, 96, from *The Horticulturist* (new series) vol. VI, 1856.

Fig. 53, 54, from *The Horticulturist*, (new series) vol. VII, 1857.

Fig. 56, from *The Horticulturist* (old series) vol. IV, July 1849.

Fig. 58, courtesy of the Connecticut Historical Soc., Hartford Conn.

Fig. 59, from *Frank Leslie's Illustrated Paper*, July 29, 1882.

Fig. 60, lithograph by J. Walton.

Fig. 61, from *Facts for Farmers*, by Solon Robinson, 1877.

Acknowledgments

200   Fig. 62, 63, from *Country Life*, June 1918. Loaned by Mrs. Judith Zlotsky.

Fig. 64, 65, from *Country Life*, Nov. 1917. Loaned by Mrs. Judith Zlotsky.

Fig. 66, from *Country Life*, Mar. 1919. Loaned by Mrs. Judith Zlotsky.

Fig. 68, from *Country Life*, Aug. 1919. Loaned by Mrs. Judith Zlotsky.

Fig. 70, drawn by Harold O. Perkins, 1932.

Fig. 72, lithograph by Geo. Hayward, for *D. T. Valentine's Manual*, 1864. Loaned by Mrs. Florence Waxman.

Fig. 75, courtesy of the Library of Congress, Washington, D.C.

Fig. 76, from *Harper's Weekly*, March 25, 1871.

Fig. 77, from *A Book of Country Sunshine*, by Clifton Johnson, 1896, p. 171.

Fig. 78, 79, from *Picturesque America*, edited by William Cullen Bryant, vol. II, 1874.

Fig. 80, by C. Rosenberry, engraved by G. R. Hall, printed by D. Appleton, N.Y.

Fig. 83, 84, loaned by Mrs. Gertrude Savage, Mansfield, Conn.

Fig. 85, from *The Horticulturist*, vol. VI, 1851.

Fig. 86, loaned by Miss Louise Wheeler, Old Mystic, Conn.

Fig. 87, from View of Mystic River and Mystic Bridge, Conn., 1879. (Map by O. H. Bailey and J. C. Hazen, Boston.)

Fig. 95, lithograph by Major and Knapp for *D. T. Valentine's Manual*, 1864.

Fig. 97, from *The Horticulturist*, vol. VII, Feb. 1849.

Fig. 98, from *The Horticulturist*, July 1846.

Fig. 100, 110, from *The Horticulturist* (new series), vol. VIII, 1858.

Fig. 101, 102, 103, 109, *The New Practical Gardener*, by James Anderson, London, 1879.

Fig. 111, from *Cottage Residences; or A Series of Designs for Rural Cottages and Villas and Their Gardens and Grounds*, by A. J. Downing, 1856.

Index